SOLD!

SOLD!

A *PROVEN*
SOCIAL MEDIA
STRATEGY
for Generating
REAL ESTATE
LEADS

SCOTT CAMERON SMITH

DARREN TUNSTALL

Huntington Media

Published by Huntington Media
8231 Camino Del Oro, Suite 6
La Jolla, CA 92037
www.huntingtonmedia.com

ISBN: 978-0-9853929-0-1

Library of Congress Control Number: 2012943512

Cover design: Teri Rider and Associates
Interior layout and typography: Teri Rider and Associates
Editing services: eFrog Press

We dedicate this book
to all real estate professionals.

Contents

Preface

ABOUT THE AUTHORS

Darren Tunstall

By experience and education, I am an entrepreneur. Before getting into real estate, I owned a freight brokerage company called Freight VIT (Very Important Transportation). The company arranged for transportation between shippers and carriers (a.k.a. truck drivers and manufacturers). By the time the company reached the third year of business, sales had quadrupled. At that time, I discovered that the trucking industry was not my real passion. I looked at my education and what transferrable skills I had and decided that I needed to get involved with real estate. I figured if I could arrange for transportation between shippers and carriers, then I could arrange for real estate transactions between home buyers and sellers. I studied to get my real estate license from the Department of Real Estate (DRE). Scott Cameron Smith, coauthor, encouraged me to consider one of the top three residential real estate companies that had great training.

In the first month after my training, I put one buyer in my car and thought to myself, "This sucks!" I did not like the idea of putting someone in my car and driving them around to show them homes. I showed that first buyer approximately sixty homes and they did not buy. I worked approximately 180 hours for free. Had they bought a home, I would have grossed approximately $69 per hour (500K*2.5% divided by 180 hours) before expenses such as royalties, administrative, transaction coordinator, and other fees. I saw this as being in the red $12,500 and spending more than a week away from my family, just because of one buyer that I decided to put in my car and just drive around. That was something I was not willing to do again!

Shortly after that experience, I recalled a statistic from the National Association of Realtors (NAR 2010, 46):

"95% of individuals between 18-44 used the internet as an information source when searching for their home."

I found that number to be staggering. Then I thought to myself, "I need to be online; that's where buyers and sellers are looking."

During that first year in real estate, I decided to learn more about the Internet while learning real estate. I built websites, blogs, connected social media networks, etc. Whatever it was that I could do to gain more experience, I would do it. Knowing the number 95% made me want to learn more. In the second year, I put some of these online strategies to work for myself. Without having a consistent online marketing schedule or a search engine business plan, I was able to bring in $3.5 million dollars of closed transactions the first year, just from blogging. I used no social media and did not spend a dime in advertising.

Currently, and just for this book, I set up an example blog site integrated with social media using the techniques in this book. The site has been up for one month. Already, I have two people under contract approved at $500K and another client at $300K. That's $1.3 million and $39,000 in potential commission. I refer all my leads to agents who do two things: close and pay me. My referral fee is 30% of the agent's gross commission. For this month, January 2012, I will have spent 66 (2 hours/day) hours blogging and social networking while earning $11,700 in gross referral commissions. That's $177 per hour. And that is without leaving my house to show homes or taking time away from my family. Of course, these numbers are unique to my situation and your results may vary due to the time, consistency, and efforts you put in to your business.

Deep down, I always knew that business could be done differently and more efficiently. I have a business degree from California State University, Fresno (CSUF) with an emphasis in marketing. I am a self-taught Internet marketing strategist and I open my arms to trial and error.

I am a proficient search engine optimization (SEO) professional, including Internet marketing planning and SEO strategy development. I consult on keyword search, content development, web traffic analytics, and link popularity services. Other strategies include content creation and optimization, link building, internal link validation, social optimization, static URL creation, headline and title optimization, analytics and statistics tracking, webmaster tools support, XML sitemaps, local listing optimization, HTML changes, dynamic optimizations, site navigation, no-follow, landing pages, cache and crawl control, and keyword research.

I have spent hundreds of hours evaluating search engines, and the architectural changes that increase a website's search engine position. These improvements do make a significant and positive change in a company's bottom line. I am driven by organic results. It is a passion of mine to have an online presence without spending a dime on advertising.

My hope is that real estate professionals will read this book and change the way they do business online.

Scott Cameron Smith

My passion has always been real estate, so when I graduated from the University of California, San Diego (UCSD) with a degree in psychology, I immediately went out and got my real estate sales license. Just as I received my license, I was accepted into law school, so I decided to attend California Western School of Law where I specialized in real estate law, contract law, and negotiation. Soon after graduation I became a California licensed real estate broker and instead of going into the practice of law, I went directly into the real estate profession.

My education and experience eventually allowed me to become involved in many aspects of residential and commercial real estate from site acquisition and analysis, development costing and project pro formas, to management and leasing. I also gained incredible experience in the foreclosure marketplace, focusing on the acquisition and sales of REO's (representing Fannie Mae, as well as disposition companies), successfully acquiring and/or negotiating short sales (as a partner in a national short sale negotiation company), and valuing, purchasing, redeveloping, and profitably selling distressed properties. In the finance industry, I was directly responsible for the loan origination, processing, and underwriting of loan production in excess of $100 million in three years.

With time, I had the opportunity to use my education, experience, and political acumen to effectively negotiate, operate, and manage many residential and commercial real estate properties and/or projects. Over the years, I gained extensive operations, management, coaching, and client service experience and eventually became a consultant for several top residential and commercial real estate firms. I was fortunate enough, over time, to garner invaluable experience in successfully recruiting, training, and coaching real estate agents in many aspects of the real estate profession including the art of lead generation and business building (e.g., getting appointments, securing listings, and effectively using leverage).

Lead generation is so critical in the building of any business, especially the real estate profession. Setting up and consistently implementing your traditional (e.g., advertising, cold-calling, door knocking, etc.) AND nontraditional (e.g., your avenues of social media) forms of lead generation will provide you with excellent and lasting results. It has been my experience, as well as my coauthor's experience, that most real estate professionals do not understand the power and reach of social media, nor do they know how to effectively use all that social media has to offer.

This is why we wrote the book...we have simply combined some of the key aspects behind successful lead generation with an easy step-by-step approach to social media that, if followed consistently, will generate quality leads. All this with little or no cost to you! How do we know? Easy...we have followed the simple process that we have presented in this book and it works!

I hope you enjoy reading this book as much as we have enjoyed writing it!

1 | Getting Started

Real estate marketing campaigns are nothing new to the focused real estate agent with a positive mind-set. The question is what marketing campaigns can a real estate agent focus on that will bring the desired results? There are several campaigns that can produce great results, but oftentimes they are not only similar to your fellow real estate agent's marketing campaign (e.g., neighborhood postcards, newspaper and magazine ads, online ads, cold-calling, door knocking, etc.), but they can be very much out of your comfort zone, extremely expensive, and/or ineffective if not applied properly.

The popularity of the Internet has created the opportunity for new avenues of effective marketing campaigns. One such opportunity lies in the realm of social media. Social media is a version of online media that embraces and encourages interactive conversation between the content creators and their audience, where people are talking, sharing, and networking together online. Traditional media presents content, but it does not allow its audience the opportunity to directly interact with or participate in the flow of the content.

Social media allows you to openly and easily share your ideas, comments, likes and dislikes, photos, videos with your family, friends, community, and business contacts. The business community has begun to recognize the tremendous value in the interactive components of social media to reach their target markets and connect on a personal level with their customers.

No matter the size of your business, social media (e.g., Facebook, Twitter, LinkedIn, and of course, blogging) can be used to start a conversation with your target market and elevate your presence and ultimately your brand. Social media is something that takes place online. It is a type of communication that takes place outside of in-person meetings, phone calls, or foot traffic. That means social media is location-independent, which makes it a valuable part of any individual's business strategy.

Content used to be something that very few people created. Reporters, TV anchors, movie directors, authors, radio DJs, and magazine editors created content, and everyone else consumed it. However, the basis of social media allows the content to be user-generated. Now everyone is a publisher, and the people who use the content are also the ones who create it.

A study released by the Pew Research Center (Hampton, et al. 2011, 12) detailed some interesting statistics on social media users and on how social networking affects our lives. As you can see in Figure 1-1, the target audience spends A LOT of time on social media each week.

	MySpace	Facebook	LinkedIn	Twitter	Other SNS
Several times a day	3%	31%	3%	20%	15%
About once a day	5%	21%	3%	13%	17%
3-5 days a week	2%	15%	4%	6%	14%
1-2 days a week	17%	17%	18%	9%	16%
Every few weeks	12%	11%	28%	12%	19%
Less often	33%	5%	35%	23%	14%
Never	29%	1%	9%	18%	5%

Source: Pew Research Center's Internet & American Life Social Network Site survey conducted on landline and cell phone between October 20-November 28, 2010. N for full sample is 2,255 and margin of error is +/- 2.3 percentage points. N for social network site and Twitter users is 975 and margin of error is +/- 3.5 percentage points.

FIGURE 1-1. Pew Research Study on social media users.

Nearly 1 out of every 3 people visits Facebook several times a day! 84% of Facebook users check in at least 1–2 days every single week.

Education distribution by social networking site platform

% of users on the following social networking sites with the following levels of education. For instance, 12% of MySpace users have a bachelor's degree.

	MySpace	Facebook	LinkedIn	Twitter	Other SNS
Less than high school	11%	5%	2%	6%	7%
High school	35%	26%	7%	16%	36%
Trade or some college	36%	34%	16%	39%	32%
Bachelor's Degree	12%	20%	37%	21%	14%
Graduate School	6%	15%	38%	18%	11%

FIGURE 1-2. Pew Research Study on the education levels of social media users.

Figure 1-2 shows that the majority of social media users are college educated. A whopping 75% of LinkedIn users have a bachelor's or graduate degree. Nearly 70% of Facebook users have some trade or college education.

As you can see, social media is highly accessible and scalable to the public, which means that social media has lots of users and offers plenty of opportunity for everyone. Because social media is easy to access, the tools for social media are easy and intuitive enough for the common person to use.

Following are more interesting statistics on social media usage (compiled by Banking.com, July 2011):

- **38,000,000** people in the US, ages 13–80, said their purchasing decisions are influenced by social media, a 14% increase in the past six months. (Source: Knowledge Networks)

- **1,000,000** people view customer service-related tweets every week, with 80% of them being critical or negative in nature. (Source: Twitter)

- **132.5** million people in the US will use Facebook this year; by 2013 the number will increase to 152.1 million. (Source: eMarketer)

- **59%** of Internet users use at least one social networking service, compared to 34% who did in 2008. (Source: Pew Internet)

- **176,000,000** US Internet users watched online video content in May 2011, an average of 15.9 hours per viewer. (Source: comScore)

- **81** minutes was the average daily use of mobile apps in June 2011, compared to 74 minutes for the web. (Source: Social Times)

- **750,000,000** monthly active users for social networking giant Facebook, up from 500 million active monthly users last year. (Source: TechCrunch)

- **12%** of US adults had an e-book reader as of May 2011, up from 6% in November 2010. (Source: Pew Internet)

You are probably thinking that this may be interesting, but how will the Internet, social media, and—more particularly—blogging increase my real estate business? Well, according to the National Association of Realtors in their most recent *Profile of Home Buyers and Sellers 2010* (Banking.com staff 2011, 12), they found that real estate agents and the Internet share a complimentary relationship and continue to be the most important resource in the home buying search process. The NAR reports that home buyers that use the Internet to search are more likely to buy their home through a real estate agent and often take steps to look at a particular property they saw online. Buyers find visuals on the Internet particularly useful—detailed information about the property for sale, pictures of the property, and virtual tours all aid the buyers. Overall 91% of buyers were very satisfied or somewhat satisfied with their home buying process. In addition, 91% of sellers reported that their home was listed or advertised on the Internet.

The NAR stated that for the last three years, 89% of home buyers used the Internet in searching for their home. Among buyers who reported using the Internet, 74% reported using it frequently. As a result of searching online, buyers often viewed the home online, found an agent, and then drove by and viewed the specific home. Interestingly, 90% of those buyers that used the Internet used an agent, compared to 73% of those buyers who did not use the Internet.

I have been a licensed real estate broker for over twenty-five years with tremendous expertise and experience in "traditional" forms of marketing residential and commercial real estate. I found the "nontraditional" forms (social media) to be confusing, overbearing (too much information), and inconsistent (information and processes that seemed to be constantly changing)! Truth is, I didn't understand the power of social media, and even if I did, I wouldn't know how to use it! I know many, if not most of you reading this book, feel the same way I did. That is when my coauthor, Darren Tunstall, called me and told me that although he was a residential agent (with not much experience), he was tired of the traditional forms of marketing real estate and had gotten involved in using social media to lead generate and market his real estate transactions. He went on to say that his social media marketing efforts resulted in over $3.5 million in closed transactions that year. He certainly had my attention and I was excited to learn more!

Obviously, the Internet and social media are positive and powerful marketing tools for any real estate agent interested in building his or her brand and capitalizing on a valuable source for lead generation. But who has time to tweet and blog and Facebook? Who has the equipment or skill to post to YouTube? We acknowledge that social media can be time-consuming, but we have integrated these social media elements into our businesses with positive results. In the next chapters, we will share with you what we have discovered, including shortcuts and simple ways you, too, can generate more leads with online social networks than you ever dreamed possible—without being chained to your computer!

2 | What is Real Estate Blogging?

An extremely viable and responsive form of social media is the use of blogging, which has created excellent results for those real estate agents that understand the concept and value of blogging.

Effective Marketing Campaign in the Community

Real estate blogging is an effective marketing campaign that can increase your visibility in your community, directly connecting you with your clients (and prospective clients), provide an excellent lead generation source, and allow you to be the authority on the subjects you choose to blog about. The best thing is that it can be extremely inexpensive!

What Is a Blog?

A blog (an abbreviated version of "weblog") is a type of website or part of a website that is (or should be) updated with new content on a **consistent** basis. Blogs feature a diary-like commentary and are maintained by an individual with regular entries of content, descriptions of events, links to articles on other websites, and other material such as graphics, video, presentations, property details, etc. The content is usually displayed in reverse-chronological order with the most recent posts featured first. The person writing the blog is the *blogger* and the information being written into the blog are called *posts*.

Blogs range from the personal to the political, and can focus on one narrow subject or a whole range of subjects. Blogs focus on a specific subject or topic, such as real estate, home staging, sports, or community events. Some are more generic, presenting links to all types of other sites and others are more like personal journals, presenting the author's daily life and thoughts.

Blog Post Examples

As we said above, blogs can be displayed in many forms about thousands of topics. Here are four examples of the types of articles that you can write:

- List Articles
- Conversation Starters
- Listings
- Community Pages

List Articles

List articles are articles that list information in an organized structure. Some examples are:

- 5 Things You Should Know About Buying a Home
- 10 Ways to Save Your Home from Foreclosure
- The #1 Reason Why You Should Short Sale Your Home

Below is an example of a list article in a real estate blog:

> **Top 4 Things You Should Know About Selling or Buying a Home**
> *Posted on February 24, 2012 by admin*

Real estate has been around for a long time. The industry is cyclical, meaning that prices go up and down, including mortgage interest rates. During this recent period, 2005 to 2012, many individuals have lost money and others have made a lot of money. Many times it depends on which side of the transaction you are on. If you are selling your home, or you are a real estate professional hired to help sell, then there are four things that you will want to understand about home buyers before moving forward.

Understand Buyers Before Selling

If you are selling property, regardless of whether you are an agent or a for sale by owner (FSBO), it is a good idea to understand what home buyers are doing to find their home in the city they want to live. **What do first-time and repeat home buyers do first?** Some of the things are listed below.

1. Look Online for Properties for Sale

All buyers, regardless of first time or repeat, look online for properties for sale. This means that if you are selling your house, then your home amenities and details should be on the Internet, preferably on a real estate website. There are some sites, such as SellByMyself.com, which is a real estate website based in San Diego, California that allows home sellers to put their home up for sale.

2. Buyers Contact an Agent

The second most common thing that buyers do when buying a home is contact a real estate agent. An agent is a huge asset to have when buying a home, especially when buying a house for sale by owner. These realty professionals will be your eyes and ears on a daily basis as the market changes. Every day there are new homes being listed on the Multiple Listing Service (MLS) sites. The really good agents also know how to track homes for sale by owners when not listed on the MLS. Typically, these can be called **pocket listings**. A true professional will also handle all negotiations, paperwork, faxing, e-mailing, etc. Buyers are looking for a deal. Agents help them get those deals. It is important to note that one of the biggest concerns that home buyers have when buying a property is *real estate commission fees*. On the buyer's side, you usually don't pay commissions; the seller pays commissions. However, even though the seller pays commission, having a selling agent versus selling your home yourself is beneficial, too. This is true because in most cases a selling agent will get home sellers 10%–16% more return versus if they were to sell their home themselves. If you are only paying 6%, then you are still ahead. Real estate is about negotiation and sometimes not being represented by the right agent will negotiate you into a loss. Do yourself a favor and contact a real estate agent. This way it is a win-win situation.

3. Buyers Contact a Bank or Mortgage Lender

The third step buyers take when purchasing a home is that they talk with their banks or mortgage lenders. In the process of searching for a home, most buyers and real estate agents know that it is pointless to look at homes until they know how much the banks will loan the home buyers; otherwise you're just driving around sightseeing. Banks and mortgage lenders usually have agents to whom they refer questions and answers. So, if you are a realty agent, or a for sale by owner, then contact the banks and let them know who you are. Provide them with your name, phone, e-mail, and the address of the home you are selling.

4. Buyers Drive the Neighborhoods

Lastly, home buyers and real estate investors drive the

neighborhoods where they want to live or invest. If you are selling your home it is a good idea to put a **For Sale** sign in your front yard, even if you are selling the home by yourself. Real estate agents commonly practice this method and it is highly effective. This way when buyers are driving through the neighborhood they know immediately that you are selling your house.

Conclusion

There are many strategies available when selling your home. The idea is to understand home buyers and their search methods when purchasing. You want buyers to find you and buy your home. The four methods that we discussed are must-haves when selling your home.

In the example above, the article had a descriptive title to explain what the article was going to be about. Because this was a list article, the number 4 was used to indicate the four things that were going to be discussed. Finally, a conclusion was used to wrap up the article. Typically, you want to also add a call to action (CTA). In other words, what do you want your readers to do next? You could have them call, click on a link, complete a form with name and e-mail, ask for a quote, buy something, etc.

More list article suggestions could be:
- Shopping for Rental Properties: 2 Types to Avoid
- Discover 5 Best Ways to Make Money in Real Estate
- 10 Things You Need to Know About House Prices
- The 5 Step Process of REO Properties into Rental Properties
- 8 Reasons Why Smart Investors Get Rich Flipping Properties

Where can you get more list article ideas? Some of the best places to start looking are in article directories such as Ezine or Article Dashboard. See what other people are writing about. Write down the titles they are using and the points that they are making in the article. Then, go back to your blog and write your own version of the article in your own words. We have included Ezine and Article Dashboard and their website addresses in the appendix.

Conversation Starters

A blog can also stimulate conversation where the blog readers will have the ability to provide their feedback, give suggestions, state opinions, and have those comments appear on the site. Conversations can also be initiated indirectly outside the blog. Later, we will discuss social networking and how to incorporate social media into your blog for the purpose of creating conversation and relationships, ultimately having buyers and sellers clicking to your site. The example below displays an article post on a blog with regards to a place a real estate agent physically visited:

The Perking Lot in San Diego Bonita

Posted on January 17, 2012 by admin

A couple of weeks ago, I checked in on Foursquare at a coffee shop in Bonita, CA in San Diego 91902. The coffee shop was called The Perking Lot. If you have never tried this coffee shop, then you need to go because it is a very good place with very good coffee.

The owner has a great since of humor. She has a sign hanging on her front door that says: Unattended Children Will Be Given Espresso and a Free Kitten.

I even took a picture of it. See below:

I had the Mexican mocha. Try visiting The Perking Lot and check in at Foursquare to share your thoughts.

One of the best tactics the real estate blogger used in the post above was incorporating a YouTube video that talked about the coffee shop, as seen in Figure 2-1. The actual check-in referenced in the article used a social media site called Foursquare (which is explained in Chapter 4). Figure 2-2 is the actual check-in at Foursquare, which consequently was posted using a smart phone.

Figure 2-1. YouTube video that was posted on the blog.

As you can see on the next page, people want to converse. The picture in the check-in clearly is a great conversation starter and people reacted to it. People are nosy, too. They will click on the picture and other links. If your profiles are set up correctly, those people will find your blog and hopefully contact you about buying, selling, or investing in real estate.

Darren Tunstall checked in to **The Perking Lot**

❝❝ Ask for a free kitten

Jan 10 via foursquare for Android

Points for this check-in:

Your first check-in at The Perking Lot!

First of your friends to check in here

Jennifer J. Jan 10
I'm bringing a toddler there, stat!

Victor S. Jan 11
Nice where can I drop off my 12 kid army lol

Ricky L. Jan 13
LOl is this real?

Darren T. Jan 14
You better believe it's real!

Figure 2-2. Foursquare check-in posted using a smart phone.

Listings

Listings are a type of post that real estate agents should be posting every day. They are the primary reason why home buyers and sellers are visiting your blog. By posting a listing that is available on the MLS, you are adding to the daily feed for the search engines to find. A listing can be as simple as including:

1. The property address, city, state, zip, and MLS number.
2. Property details including pictures, price, bedrooms, bathrooms, home size, lot size, days on the market, and other amenities and features.
3. A map pinpointing where the property is located in a given area.
4. Local market data including restaurants, parks, fitness centers, tea and coffee houses, grocery stores, etc.
5. Related articles about the area.

Below is an example of a real listings post:

1234 Example Ct., City, ST Zip (MLS # 55000XXXX)

(All data current as of 2/26/2012)

Price	$519,900
Beds	4
Baths	2 full, 1 half
Home size	2,337 sq ft
Lot Size	n/a
Days on Market	17

SELLER WILL ENTERTAIN OFFERS BETWEEN $499,900 - $519,900- VIEW! VIEW! VIEW! BEAUTIFUL SINGLE STORY- CUL-DE-SAC LOCATION- .53 ACRES- LOVELY FLOORPLAN- OPEN SPACIOUS LIVING AND SEPARATE DINING ROOM- GORGEOUS NEW KITCHEN WITH BRAND NEW CABINETRY- STAINLESS STEEL APPLIANCES- GRANITE COUNTERTOPS- ENGINEERED WOODEN FLOORS- SPACIOUS MASTER BEDROOM- REMODELLED MASTER BATH- LARGE CLOSETS- DUAL GLAZED WINDOWS- NEW LIGHTING- NO HOA- NO MELLO-ROOS- CLOSE TO FREEWAYS AND DOWNTOWN

Property Type(s): Residential / Detached, Residential / All

Last Updated	2/14/2012	Tract	Bonita
Year Built	1968	Community	Bonita
Garage Spaces	n/a	County	San Diego
Total Parking	n/a	Walk Score	26

Additional Details

CDR/Mello Roos	0.0	Home Owner Fees	0.0
Total CDR/Mello-Roos	0	Bedroom 5 Dimensions	13x13
Bedroom 4 Dimensions	14x12	Bedroom 3 Dimensions	12x10
Family Room Dimensions	18x12	Bedroom 2 Dimensions	14x11
Master Bedroom Dimensions	16x14	Living Room Dimensions	18x13
Kitchen Dimensions	15x5	Dining Room Dimensions	14x12
Parking Garage Spaces	2	Total Other Fees	0

Features

Construction	Built on Site
Cooling	Central Forced Air
Equipment Available	Dishwasher, Disposal, Range/Oven
Exterior	Stucco
Fencing	Partial
Heat Equipment	Forced Air Unit
Heat Source	Natural Gas
Laundry Location	Garage
Laundry Utilities	Gas
List Status	Active
Market Area	South Bay
Ownership	Fee Simple
Parking Garage Description	Attached
Prop Type	Residential
Property Restrictions Known	None Known

Residential Styles	Detached
Residential Unit Location	Detached
Roof	Composition
Sewer/Septic	Septic Installed
Stories	1 Story
Subject to Court/Lender Approv	No
Topography	Level
View	Mountains/Hills, Valley/Canyon
Water	Meter on Property

Location

Local Market Near Bonita in San Diego

Poppa's Fresh Fish Company
☆☆☆☆☆ based on 30 reviews - read reviews
Categories: Seafood Markets
La Mesa

Balboa Park
☆☆☆☆☆ based on 588 reviews - read reviews
Categories: Parks, Venues & Event Spaces
1549 El Prado, San Diego

Pilgrimage of the Heart Yoga
☆☆☆☆☆ based on 61 reviews - read reviews
Categories: Yoga
3287 Adams Ave, San Diego

Related articles

- The Perking Lot in San Diego Bonita (darrentunstall.com)
- Delightful Decadence: A Wine, Cheese and Chocolate Experience (imperialbeach.patch.com)
- Your Wednesday Weather Forecast (nbcsandiego.com)
- Meals-on-Wheels Greater San Diego, Inc. March for Meals Food Truck Lunch (ranchobernardo.patch.com)
- Rainfall Totals and Crash Statistics for Tuesday (lemongrove.patch.com)

Figure 2-3. Example of a listings blog post.

The example above in Figure 2-3 shows many features of a property listing including pictures, amenities, maps, local businesses, etc. Posting a listing on your blog can generate traffic to your site because it is rich in keywords, but more importantly, you are giving your visitors exactly what they want...details.

Other types of listings can include:
- Listing by zip code
- Listings by communities
- Listings by tracts
- Listings by home values
- Individual listings

The list goes on and on. If there is ever a point that you run out of ideas of what to write about, think of listings. The possibilities are endless when you list homes as your blog content.

Community Pages

Including community pages in your blog can add depth and gives the search engines an opportunity to find your site by potential buyers and sellers who are researching a particular area. Community pages can include:
- Welcoming message for that area
- Recent homes for sale in that area
- Description about the area
- Neighborhoods within the area

recent homes sold → blog idea.

Here is an example of a community page:

Homes in San Diego, La Jolla CA

Welcome to the La Jolla homes and real
estate site by San Diego Realtor, Darren
Tunstall: your only stop for finding a house in
La Jolla. Search every available home for sale
in La Jolla, CA.

As of today there are many homes and
properties for sale that are available to search
in La Jolla. The number of homes change every day, so be sure to keep coming
back to search for La Jolla homes for sale by the BIGGEST name in San Diego
real estate.

Recent La Jolla Homes For Sale

Find homes or condos in La Jolla and learn more about the community including
schools, home values, foreclosures, short sales, and more. Search all homes for
sale in La Jolla and explore the value of La Jolla real estate.

Showing properties 1–8 of 354. See more city of La Jolla real estate.
(All data current as of 2/26/2012)

$1,495,000: 1234 Example Street, City Name

4 beds, 2 full baths
Home size: 2,700 sq ft
Lot size: 10,000 sq ft
Year built: 1960
Parking spots: 4
Days on market: 3

$4,950,000: 1234 Example Street, City Name

5 beds, 4 full, 2 part baths
Home size: 5,799 sq ft
Lot size: 1.97 ac
Year built: 1995
Parking spots: 8
Days on market: 4

About La Jolla

La Jolla is an affluent, hilly, seaside resort community, occupying 7 miles of curving coastline along the Pacific Ocean in Southern California within the northern city limits of San Diego. La Jolla is surrounded on three sides by ocean bluffs and beaches and is located 12 miles north of downtown San Diego, and 40 miles south of Orange County California. La Jolla is home to a variety of businesses in the areas of lodging, dining, shopping, software, finance, real estate, bioengineering, medical practice, and scientific research.

La Jolla Neighborhoods

- La Jolla Farms
- La Jolla Shores
- La Jolla Heights
- Hidden Valley
- Country Club
- Village
- Beach-Barber Tract
- Lower Hermosa
- Bird Rock
- Muirlands
- La Jolla Mesa
- La Jolla Alta
- Soledad South
- Muirlands West
- Upper Hermosa
- La Jolla Village

Figure 2-4. Example of a community page blog post.

Buyers know the area where they would like to live. Providing community pages with details offers useful and valuable information to your readers as shown in Figure 2-4. Not only do your visitors appreciate it, but the search engines love it, too. Building out community pages will help you gain more search engine visibility and reach more home buyers and sellers.

Blogging Comments

If your blog is growing, keep up with the comments that your readers leave. Sometimes, however, this can be overwhelming if you don't have a process in place. We recommend you do the following:

- Time Block
- Reply How You Want to Be Replied To
- Pay Attention
- Don't Reply to SPAM, Trash It
- Be Consistent

Time Block

Block out certain days and/or times. For example, reply to comments on Mondays, Wednesdays, and Fridays for thirty minutes each morning or afternoon. This way you know it's on your schedule and it will get done.

Reply How You Want to Be Replied To

This really is nothing but having the right mind-set. Be positive. Engage in the conversation and readers will converse with you. You never know—it could be a potential buyer, seller, or investor. Occasionally, you will have irate readers who hate the world and decide to lash out on your blog. In these situations, it is important to be polite and patient. Sometimes human behavior wants to respond immediately with the attitude of "I told them." This is the worst thing that you can do. Be creative, but stern. And remember: reply how you want to be replied to.

Pay Attention

By paying attention, we mean read the actual comments, don't just skim over them. It is far too easy to see you have a comment and just reply with "Thanks for the comment." Many times your readers will ask you specific questions about a home, lot size, pictures, price, etc. This is a huge signal for a potential buyer or seller, so read the comments and reply accordingly.

Don't Reply to Spam, Trash It

Spam is unsolicited e-mail and in blogging situations are unsolicited or non-related comments. Ignore the junk and just trash it. It's not worth the time. Again, it's important to determine that the comment is spam by paying attention as mentioned above; otherwise you may end up approving something that you don't want posted on your blog.

Be Consistent

This reflects on time blocking. By having a schedule in place you will be able to consistently manage and reply to comments on a set schedule.

Comments are good thing. It means that people are interested in your blog and they want to communicate with you. Effectively reply to them in order gain their trust while developing your authority.

Blogging is an extremely effective marketing campaign and the great thing about blogging is that it is simple, if you know what to do. The next few chapters will explain in detail exactly what you should do to make the most out of your real estate blog. We have set forth essential steps in this book that will teach the basics of blogging and then show you methods and strategies to optimize your results.

3 | Search Engine Optimization (SEO)

What Is Search Engine Optimization?

Search Engine Optimization (SEO) is a method of increasing the visibility of a blog, web page, or website in search engines through organic search results in hopes that users will find your page without you spending a dime in advertising. SEO was considered by many to be one of the more technical roles of Internet marketing. Although this was true in the past, and still is to a degree, it is now much easier through the use of blogging service providers. Blogs have made integrating SEO much easier without having to know any programming language; just a willingness to learn the blog platform software, sometimes referred to as software as a service (SaaS). In the chapters to come we have laid out a plan for you to promote your real estate business online using real practical strategies versus learning the theory of a programming language.

One Truth About SEO

If there were one truth about SEO, it would be that it does not guarantee you to be on the first page of search engine results above the fold (before scrolling down). You are even more certain to end up down the page if you don't adhere to the simple rules that many websites and blogs were originally built with; i.e., simple metadata such as titles, headlines, descriptions, and keywords. All sites include, at the very basic level, information that tells search engines what a page is about when it is found online.

The Very Basics of SEO

At a very basic foundation of SEO, you need to provide unique information about every page on your blog. These include:

- Browser Title
- Heading Title
- Description
- Keywords

Browser Title

The browser title is the description of the page and is displayed across the top bar of the browser in the upper left corner. Browser titles are also visible on tabs and are the label when users bookmark a page as shown in Figure 3-1. The browser title should be 65 characters or less. In the example below, the browser title displays the address, city, state, zip, and MLS number as the browser title.

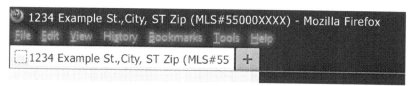

Figure 3-1. Example of a browser title.

Heading Title

The heading title, also called H1 or H2 tags (discussed in Chapter 5), is visible at the top of the page or post, summing up the page contents as shown in Figure 3-2. Typically, the title should be only one or two words. However, in real estate, we use the whole property address including city, state, zip, and MLS number. This method has proven to receive traffic because in our analytics, users query in the search engine's actual addresses. Therefore, long real estate addresses are okay to use as heading titles. An example of a heading title is:

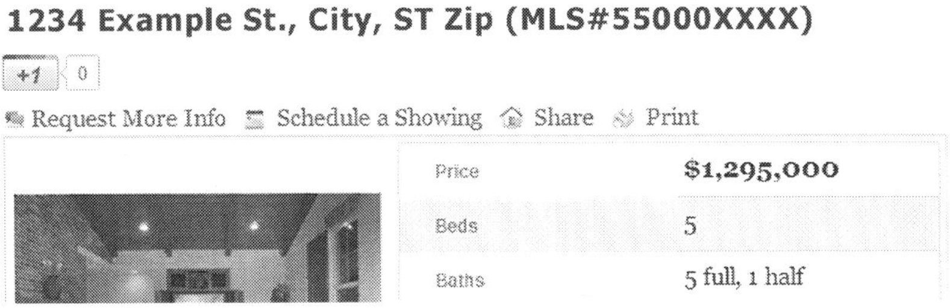

1234 Example St., City, ST Zip (MLS#55000XXXX)

+1   0

Request More Info   Schedule a Showing   Share   Print

	Price	**$1,295,000**
	Beds	5
	Baths	5 full, 1 half

Figure 3-2. Example of a heading title.

In the example below, analytics (which defines how people find you online) shows us the keywords that users type into the search engines to find a particular property:

☐	1.	(not provided)
☐	2.	site:darrentunstall.com
☐	3.	1652 las flores san marcos
☐	4.	darren tunstall
☐	5.	what is a trustee's deed
☐	6.	15753 el camino real
☐	7.	1655 santa margarita, fall brook, ca
☐	8.	chase short sale approval letter
☐	9.	keller williams
☐	10.	arizona foreclosure eviction process

Plot Rows

Figure 3-3. Keywords used in a search engine.

In the case shown in Figure 3-3, users went to search engines and typed in the following addresses and found our blog:

- 1652 Las Flores San Marcos
- 15753 El Camino Real
- 1655 Santa Margarita, Fallbrook, CA

Buyers were able to find the listings because of the use of proper heading titles and keywords, which we will talk about later in this section.

Description

The description is a brief summary, no more than 160 characters, which utilizes keywords on the page or post. In real estate, you might want to include the address, the community, the tract, and the county the property exists. Or you could use the description of the property. This description is usually visible in the search engines results page (SERP). An example is below:

16754 Georgios Wy, Ramona, CA 92065 (MLS # 120009078)
darrentunstall.com/.../mls-120009078-16754_georgios_wy_ramona_...
Feb 17, 2012 – Wonderful remodeled Ramona home in MOVE-IN ready condition! Nre granite counter-tops, travertine tile flooring and plush carpet, stainless ...

1164 Parkview Dr, Oceanside, CA 92057 (MLS # 120009006)
darrentunstall.com/.../mls-120009006-1164_parkview_dr_oceanside...
5 days ago – EQUITY SALE! Located In The Master Planned Arrowood Community, Featuring 4 Beds,3 Baths, Bonus Room, Spacious Living Room, Family ...

1850 Corte Segundo, Oceanside, CA 92056 (MLS # 120008713)
darrentunstall.com/.../mls-120008713-1850_corte_segundo_oceansi...
Feb 17, 2012 – Amazing value in Rancho Del Oro!! Corner lot and on a cul-de-sac. Double-sided fireplace adds to both the living and family rooms. Great floor ...

7463 Mission Villas Ct, Santee, CA 92071 (MLS # 120008492)
darrentunstall.com/.../mls-120008492-7463_mission_villas_ct_santee...
Feb 19, 2012 – New homes right next to Mission Trails Park! Spacious, open & light floor plans, bonus loft, lots of storage, granite kitchen, brand new designer ...

1006 Via Santalina, San Marcos, CA 92069 (MLS # 120007432)
darrentunstall.com/.../mls-120007432-1006_via_santalina_san_marc...
Feb 9, 2012 – MODEL HOME FOR SALE boasting 4 bedrooms, 3 bathrooms, downstairs bedroom & bathroom, loft, all furnishings are included.

Figure 3-4. Descriptions as they show in the search engines results page (SERP).

Below each underlined link in Figure 3-4 is a description of the property. You can either write this yourself or have it automatically generated when using the IDX tool discussed in Chapter 12.

Keywords

Keywords are terms that are relevant to your site and its individual pages. You are allowed 15 terms max before the search engines cuts off at number 16. Keywords are a critical element of SEO. An example of using keywords is:

```
<meta name="keywords" content="selling my home,sell my home,how to
sell my home,for sale by owner,buy my house, sale by owner, homes
for sale by owner, house for sale by owner, military for sale by
owner,buyer,homes for sale by owner,house for sale by
owner,military for sale by owner,mortgage loan,multiple listing
service,property,real estate,real estate broker,sale by owner,san
diego"/>
```

Figure 3-5. Example of Keywords.

We use a special plug-in called All in One SEO. We discuss this in Chapter 5 under the section "Plug-ins." The tool allows you to type in the keywords without dealing with any foreign programming language. The example in Figure 3-5 is the result of using the tool. The actual form that you would type your keywords into looks like the following:

All in One SEO Pack

Upgrade to All in One SEO Pack Pro Version

Title:	Top 4 Things You Should About Selling or Buying A Home
	54 characters. Most search engines use a maximum of 60 chars for the title.
Description:	If you are selling your home, then there are 4 things that you will want to understand about home buyers before moving or selling.
	131 characters. Most search engines use a maximum of 160 chars for the description.
Keywords (comma separated):	selling my home,sell my home,how to sell my home,for sale b
Disable on this page/post:	☐

Figure 3-6. All In One SEO form.

As you can see from the example in Figure 3-6, the All in One SEO tool is simple to use.

In Chapter 5, "Setting Up Your Blog," we discuss what you need to do, as preparation, to assemble your blog. With an Internet marketing strategy in mind, SEO takes into account how search engines operate, what people look for, and keywords and/or phrases that are typed into the engines. SEO is a constant restructuring of data both on the front end and back end of your blog. Analytics, as discussed in Chapter 12 under "Advance Customization," help you dictate the type of content you should consider presenting to your visitors. By properly incorporating basic search engine optimization strategies, you will put yourself light-years ahead of your local competition.

4 | Use of Blogging to Influence Social Media

What Is a Social Media Network?

Social media is interaction between individuals, businesses, and communities using technology to create and exchange user-driven content. In real estate, agents are making use of the Internet more than ever using social media and video hosting sites, especially on blogging platforms. The Internet and social media can help you build and maintain:

- Brand Awareness
- Communication with Your Audience
- Online Authority
- A Place for Entertainment
- Leisure Contributions
- Multimedia Management
- Reviews and Opinions

Internet User Demographics

Internet user demographics (IUD) are important in understanding why the Internet and social media play important roles in marketing your business as a real estate authority online. The National Association of Realtors reported that information sources used in a home search changed by age, as shown in Figure 4-1. The Internet was the most used source by all age groups. People between the ages of 18 and 44 were the highest users at 95%. Home buyers between the ages of 45 and 64 dropped to 87%, while those 65 and older decreased to 62%.

Age Group	18 - 24	25 - 44	45 - 64	65 or older
Internet Use	95%	95%	87%	62%

Figure 4-1. Chart data from *2010 NAR Profile of Home Buyers and Sellers*, Chicago: National Association of Realtors, 2010.

Although 87% and 62% is still a substantial amount, the point is that the aging generation is less likely to use a computer to find a real estate agent. The introduction of the information era to a baby-boomer industrial country has caused this shift in behavior. It is important to note that America has a huge population of individuals between 45 and 65. They are more concerned with holding on to their hard-earned money in a down economy rather than buying a home. And, if they happen to buy a home, statistics show that the older people get, the less likely they are to use a computer to find their next home. They are more likely to take the traditional route of contacting a real estate agent directly…and that's okay.

What you need to know is that the younger generation is coming at full speed, ready, willing, and able; they are equipped with the Internet and social media to search for their next home online. Having a well-developed search engine business plan (SEBP) will help you get in front of that generation of buyers and sellers. The market and marketing strategies are shifting into a new direction and real estate agents need to adjust accordingly.

What Is a Search Engine Business Plan (SEBP)?

Traditionally, good companies have a business plan. A business plan helps a company or individual look forward by allocating resources, focusing on goals, accomplishing missions, and helping to prepare for problems and opportunities. A standard business plan usually includes:

- Executive Summary
- Company Description
- Product or Service
- Market Analysis
- Strategy and Implementation
- Management Team
- Financial Analysis

The points above are by all means important, but how does a business plan look for real estate professionals? Unless you have a team, you don't need something complex—you need a plan that focuses on the numbers. In other words, how many people do you need to come in contact with in order to set X number of appointments? And, from those appointments, how many will actually do business with you either buying, selling, or investing in real estate? The answer to those questions means you need to answer the following questions, *in order*:

1. How much net income do you want to make?
2. How much will you spend, annually, to make the above net income?
3. How much will you pay in broker splits?
4. Will your focus be on buyers, sellers, or both?
5. What is your average commission percentage?
6. What is the average home sales price in your area?
7. What is your conversion rate after you take a listing or help a buyer find a home? These numbers are usually different.
8. What is your conversion rate from talking with a lead, either in person, phone, or web, and setting an appointment to sit down with you and talk about their real estate situation?

The answers to the eight questions above are an individual real estate agent's business plan. As it pertains to this book, the next question is: How many of these leads in question seven do you want to come from your traditional or your online efforts? This is where your search engine business plan presents itself. A search engine business plan also includes Internet social networking and social media.

Internet Social Network

A social network relates to social sciences that study social relationships within a given group of people or organizations. The goal is to understand the social interaction between the members of the groups. Each social network has its own characteristics and can be defined in many different ways. For example, a social network can be based on demographics such as age, income, gender, home ownership, employment status, and geographic location. To add more depth, you can consider psychographics that have variables related to a person's personality including values, attitudes, interests, and lifestyles.

When defining your Internet social network, you need to consider demographics and psychographics when developing your network. You can use social media to build your social network online.

Social Media

Social media is a technology-based application available on the Internet that allows people or groups to socially interact with each other. When developing your search engine business plan, you need to consider the social media sites that you want to use in order to builder your Internet social network. These can include sites such as:
- Facebook
- Foursquare
- FriendFeed
- Google +
- LinkedIn
- Pinterest
- Plaxo
- StumbleUpon

- Twitter
- Yelp
- YouTube

These are the most popular, but there are many more sites to choose from. Ideally, you want to socially interact with those that fit your business. Facebook is an excellent source because you can define your friends by gender, location, age, etc. You can even hone in on a group's particular interest. This demographic information helps you define the type of marketing that you will be pushing out to a group.

Social Media Marketing Channels of Distribution

Public marketing creates awareness. Offline, your advertising message is read through signs, postcards, letters, newsletters, business cards, personal visits, etc. The same concept of creating awareness of your message applies online through posts, tweets, videos, e-books, guides, webinars, etc. You should always be in control of how your information flows from point A to point B.

It's no mistake that we chose blogging to act as the hub of your online activity. Blogging is search engine food. There is a direct communication between blogs, social media, and the search engines. Set up properly with the right spokes on the hub, you can organically take advantage of SEO. The channels (or spokes) you should consider adding to your search engine business plan include:

Online Hubs:
- Your Blogging Platform (WordPress, Blogger, Joomla, Drupal, etc.)
- Twitter

Social Connectors (the Inverse)
- Foursquare
- YouTube (or Vlogging)
- SlideShare
- Twitter

Social Channels (the Spokes)
- Facebook
- LinkedIn
- Plaxo
- Twitter

Web Feed Management Providers

Web feed management providers allow you to connect your social media and blog together so that you can fully optimize your SEO. The providers below route your posts to the various social channels. This way, your social network is updating automatically through:
- FeedBurner
- Ping.fm

Quick Question: What's the Point?

We want to answer a quick question that we're sure has been on your mind at one time or another: What's the point of Twitter, Foursquare, Facebook, etc.?

It's fair to say that some users of social media and blogging sites truly want to stay in contact with friends and family. And by all means, that's what these companies were originally intended to do. However, due to creativity in business, savvy Internet marketers discovered that you can advertise, for free, through marketing channels to distribute real estate information with little to no hands-on involvement. At the end of the day, it's about marketing your brand and building relationships.

What's Their Purpose and How Does It Work?

Your Blogging Platform

We want to reiterate that the blogging platform you select is the hub that all information will flow to or from your social media channels of distribution. See Figure 4-2 on the following page:

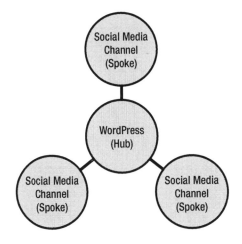

Figure 4-2. The blogging platform is the hub.

This blogging platform is the main site and provides a plug-in environment of various types of tools and templates. Consider WordPress as a content management system (CMS) where you can provide live and up-to-date information in an organized database. End users can also provide feedback in the form of a comment. For example, if a buyer or seller sees an article or home for sale on a page, they can leave their remarks for others to discuss. Hence, more free content that can be picked up by the search engines, then ultimately be found by a buyer, seller or investor.

Twitter

Twitter allows users to instantly connect to what's most important to them. It answers the question, "What are you doing?" Users can follow friends, family, experts, breaking news, and more. You are allowed to post 140 characters.

Like WordPress, Twitter also acts like a hub, but it's also a spoke for WordPress to distribute information. FeedBurner allows information from WordPress to flow to Twitter. Here's what it looks like visually. See Figure 4-3 on the following page:

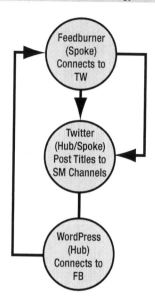

Figure 4-3. Twitter as a hub and a spoke.

As ridiculous as tweeting might sound, think about this scenario:

> You have a home for sale, so you decide to write an article about the home including address, amenities, neighborhood, etc. You title your post "1234 Elm Street, San Diego, CA 90000." Once you click "publish" your article will immediately be available to view on your blog. FeedBurner will recognize that you have a new posting and will take that article title and post it on Twitter with a hyperlink back to your original blog post.

Essentially, what you have done is created two forms of content for one article that you posted: one on WordPress and the other on Twitter. But wait, there's more!

Remember how we said Twitter also acts like a hub? From Twitter, you can connect to other social media channels. Once Twitter is connected to FeedBurner and WordPress, you will then have a connection between Twitter and your channels. See Figure 4-4 on the following page:

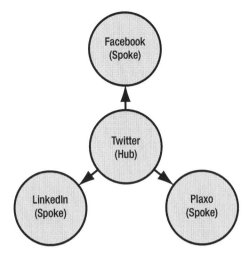

Figure 4-4. Twitter as a hub.

Because you already have the connection to FeedBurner and WordPress, your article post page, once published, will be distributed from WordPress through the channels of social media and land in front of all those connections you made on Twitter, Facebook, LinkedIn, and Plaxo.

So now, that home located at 1234 Elm Street, San Diego, CA 90000 has been sent to three other social media networks. Hence, advertising in five locations:

- Your blog
- Twitter
- Facebook
- LinkedIn
- Plaxo

Twitter is an important piece of the social media puzzle to make search engines, buyers, sellers, and investors aware of your advertising and brand. If nothing else, at least have Twitter connected.

Foursquare

Similar to Twitter, Foursquare is a location-based social networking website for mobile devices. Foursquare answers the question,

"Where are you?" Simply put, as you visit various locations (e.g., gas stations, office, grocery store, bookstore, dentist, auto parts store, etc.), you can check in and tell your network where you are in the world. Furthermore, once you check in, you can leave comments and send pictures to individuals. If a location does not exist, then you can create one. For example, when you take a new listing, you can create a location by address; name that location similar to a title in WordPress, take a picture, then click send...all from your mobile phone. Your network will be updated with where you are, but more importantly will let them know about your listing for sale, the address, and pictures.

So how is this connected to your social media channel of distribution? See Figure 4-5 below:

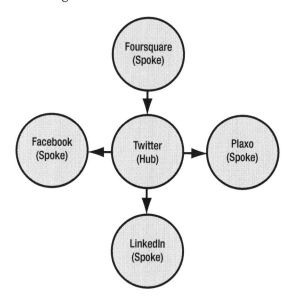

Figure 4-5. How Foursquare connects to your social network.

At this point, you might realize that your blog is nowhere to be found. In marketing real estate online, you take a different approach when using your blog. In this case you will have a posted page on your blog called "Foursquare" that has a special plug-in designed to update your blog post page every time you tell your network where you are. See the example on the following page in Figure 4-6:

Where is Darren Tunstall?

Posted on December 5, 2011 by admin

FourSquare Check-ins:

- Phở T Cali
- Eastlake Community Church
- Robeks
- Elite Gymnastics Academy
- Pretty Kitty – Chula Vista

Figure 4-6. Using Foursquare plug-in to update blog post.

One final thought on using Foursquare to connect with people in your service area. You're limited to how many people you can network with, so make it worth your while. If you live in San Diego, California, then seek out people in San Diego and only be friends with them. People will always ask if you want to be their friend.

Our rule is that if their profile is out of your area, then you don't want to be their friend. This will guarantee that you only allow your network of friends to be local, increasing your chances of helping them buy, sell, or invest in real estate.

Videos: YouTube or Video Blogging (Vlogging)

Video sharing is a process where users can upload, view, and share videos. Video has changed the culture of the Internet simply because people would rather watch than read. Connecting YouTube to your social media channels is similar to connecting Foursquare.

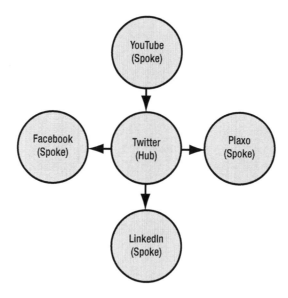

Figure 4-7. How YouTube connects to your social network.

In Figure 4-7 above, you can create a hyperlink back to your blog site by placing the final destination URL in the video description area. This allows viewers to click on the link where you want them to go. Ideally, you want viewers to come back to your site so they can look at homes for sale, read articles, and fill out forms so that you can generate buyer, seller, and/or investor leads.

Our preferred method is displayed in Figure 4-8 on the next page:

Figure 4-8. Preferred method of using video on your blog.

How do you use video in real estate? The possibilities are unlimited. Remember that house at 1234 Elm Street, San Diego, CA 90000? While you're taking pictures for the MLS and Foursquare, why not use your mobile device to shoot a quick 2–3 minute video walking through the house? From your smart phone, you can upload to WordPress as a post page and call it, "1234 Elm Street, San Diego, CA 90000 Video." If you don't have a smart phone, then use a camera and upload it when you get back to the office. Incidentally, videos can also be of you in the office giving a daily review of what's on the hotlist for the day. Other topics include pocket listings and an overview of a particular market area. Again, the possibilities are unlimited.

SlideShare

SlideShare is not necessarily a social media channel, but functions in the same way in distributing information to your social network. Users have the ability to upload and share presentations, documents, and PDF's either publicly or privately. Setting up SlideShare is similar to that of YouTube, but for presentations. Although you can network with fellow SlideShare presenters, in real estate, the focus should be on the content. Once a presentation is uploaded, regardless of the type, it is converted to text, which is well received and searchable by the search engines. Yet again, we have organic SEO.

As in the case with YouTube and vlogging (a form of blogging using videos), connecting SlideShare can be accomplished in several ways. With presentations, we like taking a two-step approach:

1. Create your presentation and upload it to SlideShare.
2. Create a post page plugging in your SlideShare presentation.

By completing these two steps, you allow for information to flow through the social media channels of distribution. See Figure 4-9:

Figure 4-9. Using SlideShare in a two-step approach.

Facebook, LinkedIn, Plaxo, and Twitter

Your social media network is primarily made up of Facebook, LinkedIn, Plaxo, and Twitter because this is where you connect with people and begin building a network (i.e., a list of potential clients). Even though we have already mentioned Twitter as a hub to connect to other channels, there is still a large following that you can connect with. Just make sure that you connect with Twitterers locally where you are practicing real estate. Twitter just so happens to be an additional hub that we recommend when connecting everything together.

Facebook is a lifestyle site. People are nosy; they want to know what other people are doing. They want to see pictures of the family, the dog, events, etc. They want to start conversation with you. This is your BIG opportunity to be a human being and show that you are not all business. You should connect with local people that you can identify with. As a lead source for business, dig into their profile and get their e-mails and phone numbers. After all, they did make friends with you. Why limit yourself to just online?

LinkedIn and Plaxo are professional network sites that you can connect with for two purposes:

1. A resource relationship (e.g., architects, lenders, escrow, etc.)
2. A business relationship (e.g., market for buyers, sellers, and investors)

Blogging Influences Social Networking

As you can see from the different social media channels that take part in your overall search engine business plan, blogging has the ability to have an influence on your social network. As information flows to your social media channels, your name, brand, company, etc., is in front of thousands of people.

Brand awareness revolves around:

- **Exposure:** As information flows through the social media channels, your blog will experience visitors, viewers, followers, fans, subscribers, and others.
- **Influence:** Your message is sent through the social media channels. Did it work? Are people offended? Do they want to take a second look?
- **Engagement:** Are people doing anything with your messages/ posts? This can come in a variety of ways including clicks,

blog comments, Twitter retweets or @replies, and Facebook wall posts.

- **Action:** This is phone calls, e-mails, and web-to-form leads. Ultimately, you want your visitors providing you with name, phone number, and e-mail.

Social Media and Lead Generation

Social media is not the sole answer to effective lead generation. Rather, it should be part of your overall lead generation model. Lead generation has four laws that real estate agents must practice daily:

1. Build a database.
2. Add to it everyday.
3. Communicate with it in a systematic way.
4. Assist all the leads you receive.

Having a good social media plan, as described earlier, will cause thousands of messages to be seen by thousands of people. It is an effective way of organically advertising and will bring in leads.

It's important to note that the first two tasks—building a database and adding to it everyday—are part of your online business. The second two—communicating with it in a systematic way and assisting in all the leads you receive—are offline, and this is where the trained real estate agent begins. Despite popular belief, just because you are on the Internet does not mean that you will be overwhelmed with leads. You need to do a lot of time-tested traditional offline work to build solid relationships.

Call to Action:
1. Get a Twitter username.
2. Set up accounts on Foursquare, Facebook, LinkedIn, YouTube, SlideShare, Plaxo, etc.
3. Write titles of potential blog posts and put them in a spreadsheet.
4. Develop an annual, monthly, weekly, and daily social media plan of action.

Tools and Resources

- Twitter: http://www.twitter.com
- Foursquare: http://www.foursquare.com
- YouTube (or vlogging): http://www.youtube.com
- SlideShare: http://www.slideshare.net
- Facebook: http://www.facebook.com
- LinkedIn: http://www.linkedin.com
- Plaxo: http://www.plaxo.com

5 | Setting Up Your Blog

Blogging is the heart of your social media efforts. In the preceding chapters we have discussed what real estate blogging is and how blogging can influence your social media network. Even though the act of blogging is simply writing, we have learned that the platform you use and the way you set up your blog are critical components to your success in connecting with clients and your target communities.

This chapter focuses on four steps to have you blogging by the end of the day:

1. Get a domain name.
2. Get web hosting.
3. Install your blog platform.
4. Set up your blog.

Domain Names

A domain name is where your blog lives on the Internet. It's your blog uniform resource locator code, popularly known as the URL address. A URL will tell a computer where a resource is and how to access it. For example, http://www.iAgentc.com, which incidentally is where we recommend you buy your domain name. Your blog's domain name should be unique to you or the farm area in which you serve.

For real estate agents, owning yourname.com (your own domain name) is the key to establishing your identity on the Internet. Buyers and sellers buy YOU, the agent, not the company or your broker.

Five Features When Selecting a Domain Name

1. Length
2. Easy to Remember
3. Niche Related
4. Dashes are Okay
5. .com is Best

Let's explain these five features in more detail:

1. **Length:** Shorter is better, but in real estate, geo-specific content is the key. We recommend either one or two syllable words. It rolls off the tongue better and is great to remember when directing traffic.

2. **Easy to Remember:** If users cannot remember your domain name, then they won't find you from the domain name itself. And that's not good for search engine marketing. Keep your domain short and simple. One syllable is ideal, but two is okay.

3. **Niche Related:** This is target marketing. Don't forget, geography in real estate is considered a niche area, but it can also apply to other types of niches. Ideally, you will want to conduct a keyword analysis before deciding on a domain name. The Google Keyword Tool is one of the better tools and will get you started in the right direction. Using keywords in your domain name will help to improve your overall SEO. For example, if an individual searches for a home in Austin, Texas, what would users type into the search engines to find their results? In the following figure we typed "Austin Texas homes" and the keyword tool provided us with popular search terms that users actually typed into the search box. As a

result, keyword ideas that could be used as domain names are provided. Search engine companies collect this data from users after they use the search box when surfing the Internet. This data is the best tool to help you decide on a domain name other than yourname.com. See the example in Figure 5-1.

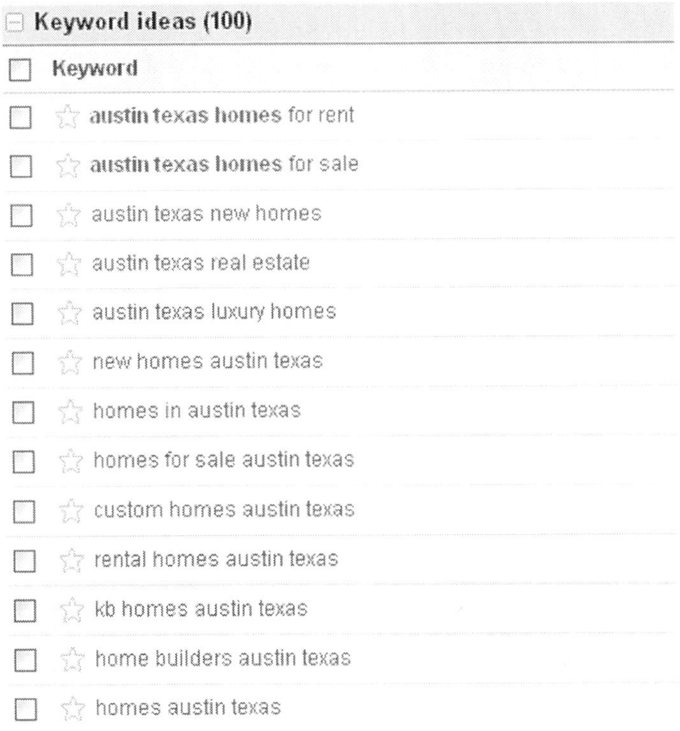

Keyword ideas (100)

- Keyword
- austin texas homes for rent
- austin texas homes for sale
- austin texas new homes
- austin texas real estate
- austin texas luxury homes
- new homes austin texas
- homes in austin texas
- homes for sale austin texas
- custom homes austin texas
- rental homes austin texas
- kb homes austin texas
- home builders austin texas
- homes austin texas

Figure 5-1. Use of Google Keyword Tool to choose a domain name.

4. **Dashes are Okay:** Search engines don't mind dashes. In fact, they behave a lot like grammar police when reading content on the web. That's why they give us the option of "Did You Mean" when we misspell a word or phrase. Words are recognized by the search engines as separate terms when they have a dash. Dashes (a.k.a. hyphens) are treated as a space between words. For example, if you are located in Austin, Texas and you want to secure the domain name http://www.austintexas.com and found out it was already registered to someone else, it would be okay to secure http://www.austin-texas.com or http://

www.austin-tx.com or some other variation with dashes. As a result, you have a small opportunity to capitalize on SEO using dashes because "austintexas" is a misspelled word and will not be recognized. In fact, as you can see in Figure 5-2, you will have the option of "Did you mean: austin texas."

Figure 5-2. Example of Google search results for misspelled words.

As it pertains to SEO, the search engines are looking for grammatically correct sentences and/or words.   Austin-Texas is considered a grammatically correct word and the search engine will recognize what that user is trying to find. Thus, it can be used as a domain name.

As a side note, if you do decide to use dashes and you want to promote that domain name offline—on a sign, for example—then tell people to use the dash. For example, the domain name buy-619.com. Make signs that spell out "Buy Dash 619" and print the domain name underneath it. See below. Trust us, viewers will get it because now they are telling their brain what to do. It's called human behavior and we are creatures of habit.

HOMES FOR SALE
Buy Dash 619
www.buy-619.com

Consequently, in this example, it would be a good idea to secure the domain name buydash619.com, just in case you have an individual who takes domain names literally.

Real Example

In the figure below we show you an example of a real and available (at this time) domain name using three words: home, Austin, and Texas. In our opinion, as it relates to SEO, this is a great domain name (and it's available!) because it capitalizes on several words. We'll break this down for you in Figure 5-3:

Figure 5-3. Checking the availability of a domain name to purchase.

First exact phrase: "home austin texas." If you search for that exact phrase in the search engines (just use quotes around your phrase to do an exact search), as of this writing, Google returned 4,950,000 results. See Figure 5-4a below:

Figure 5-4a.

Second exact phrase: "home austin." Google returned 955,000 results. See Figure 5-4b below:

Figure 5-4b.

Third exact phrase: "austin texas." Google returned 41,700,000. See Figure 5-4c below:

Figures 5-4a-c. Google search results used for choosing a domain name.

We could break this down to individual words, but that would be too much. Not only that, a word like "home" is such a broad term that you will get many types of results that may or may not be related to the location you are trying to market to and the results will be random, some of which may or may not relate to real estate. This random result is true for all the words in the figures above.

A good search engine business plan (SEBP) will help you to optimize your authority and brand online and will consider specific product/service details and location. Be sure to review the search engine marketing and optimization chapters to learn more about this subject.

5. **.com is Best:** .coms are the best because they are the most recognizable by Internet users. More often than not someone will say, "Go to yada-yada-yada.com." In general, users will automatically try the .com first in a search because we have been conditioned to do so. You might as well give them what

they want and secure the .com. However, we also recommend securing all extensions (.net, .tv, .info, .me) when developing your authority and brand identity online. The last thing you want is another real estate professional capitalizing on your hard-earned SEO strategies. Protect your space.

Why Have Multiple Domain Extensions?

Multiple domain extensions are important to your overall search engine business plan. If you are willing to truly build your online presence and develop your authority online, then you need to secure all these extensions. Below are the reasons why:

.com Domain Names

- .coms are the most popular domain name extension worldwide.
- Necessary for seeking high visibility on the Internet.
- Can be secured by anyone.

.net Domain Names

- Next-best option when .com is not available.
- Can be used from Internet communications or related services.
- Secure when buying .com to protect your online brand identity.

.info Domain Names

- Often linked with websites and blogs providing information.
- Best for business organizations and individuals.
- Recognized worldwide.

.me Domain Names

- This domain is about you and your product or service. As an agent, this is important because people buy you, not your company or broker.
- Perfect for blogs, resumes, and other types of personal pages.

.tv Domain Names

We will discuss how to use your blog after setting it up. Part of that topic will be the use of videos and other media as part of your search engine business plan. The .tv domain name extension will apply to this section, but here are a few reasons why you should secure the .tv domain names:

- Popular for multimedia websites and blogs.
- Great for launching your own Internet TV channel.
- Excellent when videos are present on your blog.

Blog Hosting

Choosing a blog hosting company is important depending on your level of experience and expertise among other features and benefits. If you are not comfortable with technical installation, then choose a company that does most of the work for you. There are hundreds, maybe thousands, of hosting companies that meet the needs of different types of people. As real estate professionals, you don't have time to learn how to be a programmer or software developer as it's not part of your job description.

Features to Look For in a Hosting Company That Specialize in Blogs

- FREE Setup
- FREE Software
- 24/7 Phone, E-mail and Web Support
- Unlimited Storage and Bandwidth
- 24/7 FTP Access
- Data Centers
- Daily Backups
- Breed Routers and Servers
- Website Statistics (or Analytics From Search Engines)
- FREE E-mail Addresses
- Google Webmaster Tools
- FAQs
- Choice of Operating System (Linux or Windows)

Added Bonuses Offered by Blog Hosting Companies

Some providers specializing in real estate blogs offer added bonuses that can complement your search engine business plan at least for a period of time. For example, some SEBP programs incorporate the use of Google AdWords or Yahoo! Advertising Solutions. These are advertising programs that you can use to help boost your overall website traffic. Some web-hosting providers offer free credit including Facebook Ad Credits. These bonus programs can be a good way to help you get started with search engine marketing. The company that we use, http://www.iAgentc.com, currently offers the following credits (displayed in the sidebar under "All Plans Include"):

- Free $100 Google AdWords Credit
- Free Up to $100 Bing™ / Yahoo! Search Credits
- Free $50 Facebook Ad Credits
- Fotolia Photo Credits

Installing Your Blog

Installing your blog has never been easier. As we said earlier, there are many blogging platforms you can use to build your blog. Although WordPress is not the only option, we will be using it as the vehicle to discuss how to create a blog. There are two ways to install your blog:

1. WordPress Web Hosting by iAgentc.com (Recommended)
2. Installing WordPress on Your Hosting Account

WordPress Web Hosting by iAgentc.com (Recommended)

The WordPress web hosting package installation is seamless. There, you can harness the combined power of WordPress and iAgentc web hosting to create your own personal, state-of-the-art blog. The WordPress publishing platform has thousands of free plug-ins, hundreds of free themes, and is completely customizable, while iAgentc hosting is powered by grid technology, which spreads traffic spikes across multiple servers so your site is always up and running at top speed.

To start installation, do the following:

1. Go to iAgentc.com.
2. Log in or create an account.
3. Secure a domain name (yourname.com and .net).
4. Mouse over web hosting.
5. Click WordPress blog hosting.
6. Click deluxe plan.
7. Add to cart and check out.
8. Go to account manager.
9. Click launch next to the hosting account you want to use.
10. Follow the instructions on the screen to finish setup.

Installing WordPress on Your Hosting Account

There are two steps to installing WordPress on your hosting account:

1. Install Hosting
2. Install WordPress on your Hosting Account

Install Hosting

Installing WordPress on your hosting account requires that you have a hosting package in place first. If you don't, then go to iAgentc.com and do the following to secure hosting:

1. Go to iAgentc.com.
2. Log in or create an account.
3. Secure a domain name (yourname.com and .net).
4. Click on web hosting.
5. Select deluxe plan.
6. Add to cart and check out.

It may take up to 24 hours for your account to be set up. Our experience has been quick. We've seen set up only take 15 minutes many times. Be patient and check back often. If, for whatever reason, the installation takes longer than 24 hours, call iAgentc's customer support. They have a 24/7 support department, where you can talk with a live person to help you get your site up and running.

Install WordPress on Your Hosting Account

After installation of your hosting account is complete, do the following to install WordPress:

1. Log in to your account manager.
2. Click web hosting.
3. Next to the hosting account you want to use, click launch.
4. From the content menu, select value applications.
5. Click WordPress.
6. Click install now. (**NOTE**: The install now button displays only when the selected value application is compatible with one of more hosting plans in your account.)
7. Select the domain name you want to use.
8. Enter a database description and password, and then click next.
9. Choose an unused installation directory, and then click next. For example, if you want your WordPress website to display when someone goes to yourdomainname.com/blog, then blog is the installation directory. (**NOTE**: If you want your WordPress website to display when someone goes directly to your domain name, remove any text from this field and leave it empty.)
10. Enter the admin name, admin password, e-mail, and blog title for your WordPress installation.
11. Click finish.

Top Things to Know When Setting Up Your Blog

Now that you know what to look for in a web hosting company, it's time to secure and start the set-up process— essential for creating a blog. There are several types of blogging programs to use and we will always choose WordPress, hands down! The WordPress publishing platform has thousands of free plug-ins, hundreds of free themes, and is customizable. WordPress allows you to optimize your search engine business plan in the search engines and across top social media channels while having direct communication with your visitors. Of course, you could also use other blog platforms such as Joomla, Drupal, Blogger, etc. Who you use depends on your comfort level.

Accessing Your Dashboard

Initially, accessing your site is tricky because it is new to you. Having said that, there are two ways of accessing the dashboard:

1. Go to your domain name (yourdomain.com) and click on site admin. By default, your blogging platform typically puts this in one of the sidebars. It is usually located at the lower right. If you change widgets then chances are this will go away. Typically, this will only work on your first log in or until you change widgets.

2. Go to yourdomain.com/wp-login.php (if you're using WordPress). If your domain name is http://www.home-austin-texas.com, then you would type http://www.home-austin-texas.com/wp-login.php. This will take you to your log in page. It will look something like Figure 5-5 below.

Figures 5-5. Wordpress log in page.

You will need to log in so that you can fully optimize your sites' settings, otherwise marketing will be difficult.

Settings

Settings include:
- Site title
- Taglines
- E-mail addresses
- Time zone
- Date format
- Time format
- Week starts on

These settings are important to your search engine business plan for several reasons. The *site title* will be displayed to the search engines as a header code. More specifically it will be identified as a H1. Without being too technical, search engines look for document structure and they look for sites that are well planned with an organized hierarchy. These headers typically go six levels deep. For example:

Heading 1 Tag (H1)

Heading 2 Tag (H2)

Heading 3 Tag (H3)

Heading 4 Tag (H4)

Heading 5 Tag (H5)

Heading 6 Tag (H6)

Search engines are attracted to headers and you need to use them, starting with your site title. Fortunately, you don't need to know how to use HTML code to incorporate the headers. Thankfully, all you need to know is how to use WordPress and it will write the code for you.

The *tagline* is a short description of what your blog is about. A unique selling proposition (USP) or slogan is best in this area. This will be displayed on the home page. See example below:

> ### San Diego Realtor | $20 Million a
> ### Year in San Diego Real Estate Sales

The *e-mail address* is important because this is where information will be sent when visitors complete your forms.

The *time zone, date format, time format,* and *week starts on* really have no impact on search engine marketing. It's just a nice way of organizing your blog and showing that it is current with time, dates, and calendars. At least the date and time will be correct when people comment on one of your posted articles or homes for sale.

Permalinks

Found under settings, permalinks is one of the most overlooked settings by users. It is critical that permalinks are set appropriately before creating pages, posts, or connecting to your social media channels.

A permalink is a visual way of identifying your pages and posts as it is presented in the URL address bar. By default, permalinks are set with an "ugly" address that looks like http://example.com/?p = N. The N is replaced with an ID (i.e., 123).

Instead, you want a custom structure to read your site using a search engine optimization approach. As it relates to real estate, you want to optimize your results on the search engines using what home buyers, sellers, and investors are looking for such as specific details about properties like addresses, streets, locations, schools, zip codes, etc.

We recommend setting your permalink settings to / % postname % /. This will change the URL visual address to the title of your page or post. For example, if you have a home listed at 1234 Elm Street, San Diego, CA 90000, the URL would show:

http://www.yourdomain.com/1234-elm-street-san-diego-ca-90000

Do you know how important this is? Think about it: displayed are the street number, street name, city, state, and zip code. You can even add other details such as the agent name, county, and home features. It is unlimited! This is what we mean by optimizing your pages for the search engines.

At the very least, you need to customize your permalinks, otherwise you will lose a lot of search engine momentum and your work will be a waste of time and money.

Post Categories

Post categories are a unique and organized method of creating a hierarchy that allows visitors to search your site accordingly. It's like creating folders in a pullout cabinet in your office, except online it's referred to as root folders and subfolders. By default, WordPress post categories are "uncategorized." Before posting or creating pages, you should have a category called "real estate."

What's even better is that you can have subcategories. For example, in real estate, subcategories can be "residential" or "commercial." To add more depth, you can create another subcategory under residential, like "short sales" or "foreclosures." Your post would then include:

Tagged with: real estate, residential, short sale

We also recommend taking another approach using location details as part of your category tags such as city, state, zip, and communities. For example:

Tagged with: real estate, california, san diego, 91915, eastlake greens

In the example above, "real estate" would be the main category, and then California the first subcategory. San Diego would be the second subcategory, 91915 the third subcategory, and Eastlake Greens as the fourth subcategory.

In this situation your visitors will benefit because now they can search for homes by state, city, zip code, or community. Do you see how the possibilities are unlimited? Each one of these is searchable on your site and by the search engines. Your URL address will then read something like this:

http://www.yourdomain.com/tag/real-estate/california/san-diego/ ca/91915/eastlake-greens

Search engines use both tags and categories interchangeably. It's content that is the key and by incorporating geo-specific content, you will be optimizing your search engine business plan.

Writing Settings

The most important thing here is to set your default post category to anything but uncategorized. Might we suggest "Real Estate"?

Discussion Settings

Comments are imperative to your site when positioning yourself as the authority in your field. Discussions can be a free source of content if you allow users to comment on your site. This is at your discretion. Just make sure that you can review a comment before it goes live on your site. You can either approve or disapprove. Search engines see these comments as activity and unique content on your site and will post it to the search engine results page. When an Internet surfer or buyer or seller sees that comment in the results page, they might click on it and arrive at your blog.

Themes

Themes control the appearance of your blog. It is the overall look and presentation of how your site is displayed to buyers, sellers, and investors as well as other real estate professionals. In real estate, appearance is extremely important because buyers and sellers want good visual displays. What does that mean? From a buyer's perspective, they want pictures of homes! In the *Profile of Home Buyers and Sellers 2010* report issued by the National Association of Realtors—the voice of real estate—it states that "for the last 3 years, approximately 90 percent of home buyers used the Internet in their home search." As a result of searching online, "buyers often walked through the home viewed online, found an agent, and drove by and viewed the home. 85% of home buyers found photos very useful on websites. See Figure 5-6 below:

Value of Website Features	Very Useful
Photos	85%
Detailed Information About Properties For Sale	83%
Real Estate Agent Contact Information	61%
Interactive Maps	43%
Neighborhood Information	40%
Pending Sales/Contract Status	33%
Detailed Information About Recently Sold Properties	30%
Information About Upcoming Open Houses	21%

Figure 5-6. Value of Website Features.

These features are important when developing a plan of how your site will be used and the way it is presented. Most top companies know the value of photographs and incorporate them into their sites. Just look at companies like Trulia and Zillow. Themes will enable you to choose your type of appearance or you can have a custom theme developed.

Plug-ins

Plug-ins help you develop the functionality of your blog. By now, it's safe to say that there is a plug-in for almost anything. As there are many, the ones that you will absolutely need before going live are the following:

All in One SEO Pack

All in One SEO Pack optimizes your real estate blog for search engines. This tool will enable you to customize your title, description, and keywords for each post or page that you publish.

Duplicate Post

The duplicate post allows you to create a draft copy of a post or a page. This copy is important in real estate if you have many neighborhoods in your service area. Once you set up a page or post, you can then duplicate that page/post to keep everything uniform if you're not using templates.

Exclude Pages from Navigation

The exclude pages plug-in includes the check box "include this page in menus." You can choose to have it in your blog's navigation or not. If you uncheck it, the page will not appear.

Google Analytics for WordPress

The Google Analytics for WordPress plug-in enables you to track your blog easily and is a rich resource for metadata including title, description, and keywords, which we will discuss later.

Google XML Sitemaps

The Google XML sitemap plug-in will generate a unique XML sitemap which will help search engines like Google, Yahoo!, Bing, and Ask.com to improve the indexing of your website.

Link Library

The link library plug-in is used to create a page on your website that will contain a list of all of the link categories that you have defined inside of the links section of the WordPress administration, along with all links defined in these categories. The user can select a subset of categories to be displayed or not displayed.

WP-Leads

The WP-Leads plug-in allows you to combine the WordPress registration and commenting processes with popular lead management tools, such as MailChimp, Constant Contact, and Salesforce.

RSS Poster

The RSS poster allows you to publish full articles from your preferred RSS feeds to your blog so that you can make valuable information available to your visitors and social media network.

Local Market Explorer

The local market explorer plug-in allows WordPress to load data from a number of neighborhood-related APIs to be presented on a single page or within your own pages/posts. The different modules that this plug-in contains are as follows:

- Real Estate Market Stats
- Real Estate Market Activity
- Schools
- Walk Score
- Yelp
- Local Classes
- Colleges
- Realtors

Call to Action

1. Get a domain name.
2. Get web hosting.
3. Install WordPress.
4. Set up.
5. Write your search engine business plan.

Tools and Resources

- Domain names, hosting, and WordPress installation: http://www.iAgentc.com.
- http://www.yourdomain.com/wp-login.php to start setting up your blog.
- http://WordPress.org/support/ for getting started and forums.
- http://codex.WordPress.org/Main_Page for the WordPress online manual.

6 | How to Use Your Blog and Social Media Tools

Time Block Your Way to Success

Before you start using your blog to distribute information to your social media network, we want to stress that when operating any business online or offline, regardless of industry, you must focus on protecting the time that you spend when building your book of business.

In real estate, traditional lead generation is typically done from 9:00 a.m. to 11:00 a.m. Some of the tasks to be accomplished during this time are:

- Phone calls
- Sending letters, postcards, brochures
- Drop-bys (visiting a lead physically)
- Door knocking

As obvious as this might sound, without lead generation, you have no leads. As a result, you have no business.

We encourage you to continue to practice the lead generation task above while including Internet lead generation as part of your daily tasks to drum up more leads.

Be the Content Machine

Being the content machine means to take a systematic, action-oriented goal approach to generating leads online. Where there is a system to stay in touch with leads, clients, and resources after they are entered into your pipeline, there is also a system for disseminating your information to the Internet so that new leads and resources will be influenced to want to learn more about you and your business.

When we present blogging and social media to real estate agents, one common question is often asked: "Will you give me a list of the things to do?" These requests have encouraged us to develop an Internet marketing schedule (IMS). The IMS allows you to organize your daily, weekly, and monthly activities while developing your own content factory.

Building a Content Factory

There are four essential phases to building a content factory:
- Phase 1: No-Touch Preparation and Circulation
- Phase 2: Low-Touch Preparation and Circulation
- Phase 3: High-Touch Preparation and Low-Touch Circulation
- Phase 4: High-Touch Preparation and Circulation

Phase 1: No-Touch Preparation and Circulation

No-touch content is automatically posted to your blog and is practiced daily at your preferred frequency per day. There are primarily two types:

Syndicated News
Syndicated news is available through the use of web syndication, where website material is offered for others to use via posting tools. It is often recognized by the terms RSS, XML, or ATOM feeds. Typical icons look like the one in Figure 6-1:

Figure 6-1. An example of an RSS feed icon.

Syndicated news is by far the easiest to set up. More specifically, really simple syndication (RSS) allows you to publish recent work such as news headlines, audios, video blog posts, and social media entries. RSS feeds benefit publishers and blog owners by letting them share syndicated content automatically. Using the RSS poster tool that we mentioned in Chapter 5, "Setting Up Your Blog," you will be able to distribute valuable news and information to your blog visitors and social media network. Other blog owners can also find your information useful and place RSS feeds on their site, which will ultimately provide a link back to your site.

Other People's Blogs (OPB)

Buyers, sellers, and investors are consistently looking online. Remember, approximately 89% of home buyers and sellers are going to the Internet to look for real estate information before they ever talk to a real estate professional. During their search for real estate information, they often ask questions. Usually, these questions are on another blog site. Through RSS feeds, trackbacks, and pingbacks (which are types of linkback methods that authors can use to request notification when someone links to their article), you can post that same information on your blog as additional and informative content while giving credit where credit is due.

Phase 2: Low-Touch Preparation and Circulation

Low-touch content takes a little preparation to develop and is posted weekly. There are primarily four types:

Your Own Editorials (YOE)

Part of your daily task should be to read what others are writing. Then, after you read the article, give your opinion or review what you just read. Known as editorializing, you can create some great, unique content that is helpful to others. An example could be as simple commenting on a local business:

> There was an insightful article today on finding the right yoga studio in La Jolla, CA. The article said that La Jollans loved hitting the gym. The author went on to say that when choosing yoga, you need to focus on a style that best suits your physical needs. He mentioned Bikram and Vinyasa. There are other styles too that are worth mentioning, including Ananda, Anusara, Ashtanga, Iyengar, Kali Ray TriYoga, and more. Try yoga today. There are several in the La Jolla neighborhood. For starters, look at La Jolla Yoga Center. They offer many options, amenities, and yoga styles. The studio is also great for beginners.

Your Own News (YON)

Create a buzz on your own news in the areas that you serve. As a real estate professional, you have so much to report to your audience. For example, use the MLS to report lows, highs, and averages for homes sold in a given area during a specified period of time. Just pull the report and write about the numbers. An example is a post on existing home sales. In this case, RSS was used to write the post shown in Figure 6-2:

Existing-Home Sales Down, Higher Than a Year Ago

Posted on January 4, 2012 by admin

+1   0

Washington, DC,
October 20, 2011

Existing-home sales were down in September on the heels of a strong gain in August, but remain well above a year ago, according to the National Association of Realtors®.

Total existing-home sales¹, which are completed transactions that include single-family, townhomes, condominiums and co-ops, declined 3.0 percent to a seasonally adjusted annual rate of 4.91 million in September from an upwardly revised 5.06 million in August, but are 11.3 percent above the 4.41 million unit pace in September 2010.

Figure 6-2. Example of a blog post that was generated by RSS.

Your Own Post (YOP)

Your own post relates to your own news. The difference is something that can be said on the fly. For example, you just left a listing appointment and sealed the deal. Take a picture of the house using your smart phone and upload it your site immediately. Literally minutes after getting signatures you can post to your audience to view.

Your Own Videos (YOV)

We put your own videos under low-touch preparation because this could be short and sweet. For example, the same report that you pulled from the MLS you could present in a video. Just turn your camera around and shoot the video. Upload it once you're finished. Don't worry too much about the quality. People want to work with "real" people. As long as you look professional and are sincere, people will listen because you are the authority.

Phase 3: High-Touch Preparation and Low-Touch Circulation

High-touch content is more hands-on and adds a little more time. The content is generated and posted monthly. There are primarily four types:

Guides

Guides are for advisory purposes only. They are meant to lead the way in helping buyers, sellers, or investors accomplish something. Guides can be categorized many ways and they come in many available forms, meaning you can create them on your own, and we suggest you write your own guides, or you can buy them. Just to name a few:

- Home Buying
- Home Selling
- Design and Decorating
- Financing
- Foreclosure
- Moving
- Renting
- Short Sale

Presentations

Naturally, a presentation is generally given when attending a seminar. They are really the short version of your guides, only pointing out the major details. The purpose of the presentation is for SEO and is free to all users. These presentations can then be uploaded to SlideShare. Set up your blog so that the presentations will travel through your social media channels and will reach your network.

E-books

An e-book is somewhat similar to a guide. It is information that is made available immediately and can easily be distributed to your readers. However, unlike a guide, an e-book is purely for lead generation. Visitors to your site must complete your form before receiving your e-book. This ensures that you get their name, phone, and e-mail. Below is a set of simple steps to create your own e-book:

1. Choose a topic that you are familiar with.
2. Make an outline.
3. Write your e-book.
4. Get feedback by having others read it.
5. Add photos.
6. Convert to PDF.

Videos

Videos are a visual way of displaying your presentation with voice-over or just you and the camera. Videos are offered to your visitors for free. Again, when properly connected, you upload and distribute your videos to YouTube or Dailymotion in order to circulate throughout your network.

Phase 4: High-Touch Preparation and Circulation

High-touch content is hands-on and adds more time. The content is generated and posted monthly. There is primarily one type of high-touch content:

Webinars

The point of webinars is to provide good information and to generate leads. Ideally, you want people to complete a registration form agreeing that they will join the webinar. The related material is your presentation information. We presented this vehicle in phase 3 as free content. Learning styles are different. Some people would just rather have the presentation read to them in the form of a webinar.

If you are thinking that you don't have time to do webinars, don't worry. Most good companies like GoToMeeting allow you to record your webinars. You only have to do it once, and then put it on your site for visitors to register.

Each phase in our plan is systematically laid out annually so that you can incorporate it into your overall search engine business plan. See example below in Figure 6-3:

Months		January				February				
Weeks	1	2	3	4	5	6	7	8	9	10
Content Marketing										
Phase 1: No-Touch Preparation and Distribution										
Syndicated News										
Other People's Blogs (OPB)										
Phase 2: Low-Touch Preparation and Distribution										
Your Own Editorials (YOE)										
Your Own News (YON)										
Your Own Post (YOP)										
Your Own Videos (YOV)										
Phase 3: High-Touch Preparation with Low-Touch Distribution										
Guides										
Presentations										
E-books										
Videos										
Phase 4: High-Touch Preparation and Distribution										
Webinars										

Figure 6-3. Example of annual online marketing plan.

In the figure above, content is laid out in phases and should reflect what's in your Internet marketing schedule. At the top you see months and weeks. The idea is to schedule your activities for the year, month, and week. This helps to meet your year-end goals. For example, annual goals could be:

Phase: 1

- 180 Posted Syndicated News
  - *Auto-posted every other day*
- 185 Posted Other People's Blogs
  - *Auto-posted every other day*

Phase 2

- 52 posted of Your Own Editorials (YOE)
  - *Once every Monday*
- 52 posted of Your Own News (YON)
  - *Once every Tuesday*
- 52 posted of Your Own Post (YOP)
  - *Once every Wednesday*
- 52 posted of Your Own Videos (YOV)
  - *Once every Thursday*

Phase 3

- 12 Guides
  - *Work on over 4 weeks, then release.*
- 12 Presentations
  - *Work on over 4 weeks, then release.*
- 12 E-books
  - *Work on over 4 weeks, then release.*
- 12 Videos
  - *Work on over 4 weeks, then release.*

Phase 4

- 12 First-time Webinars
  - *Work on over 4 weeks, then release.*

Type of Content That Buyers, Sellers, and Investors Want

Now that you know what types modules there are when building a content factory, it's time to talk about the type of content that buyers, sellers, and investors want. Just for starters, we happen to know a few:

- What is the quickest way to buy a home?
- Where is a cheaper area near {your area} to buy a home?
- How do you buy a home and get cash out of the deal?

The topics above are just the tip of the tip of the iceberg. People are also looking for information in the following categories:

- Real Estate
- Agents/Realtors
- Building a Home
- Buying
- Commercial Construction
- Commercial Property
- Condominiums
- Foreclosures
- FSBO
- Green Real Estate
- Home Staging
- Homes
- Investing
- Land
- Leasing/Renting
- Marketing
- Mortgage Refinance
- Moving/Relocating
- Property Management
- Selling

As you can see, the potential is limitless. Using your blog can be as simple as long as you have a system in place. Time blocking allows you to schedule time so that you will have a schedule to write articles, make videos, put together presentations, comment on other people's blogs, report the news, conduct webinars, and more. By combining a schedule with different types of content for your readers, you will be well on your way to generating real estate leads.

7 | Marketing Your Brand

What Is a Brand?

The American Marketing Association defines a brand as a "name, term, design, symbol, or any other feature that identifies one seller's goods or service as distinct from those of other sellers." (American Marketing Association 2011) The concept of brand came simply as a way to tell one person's cattle from another and was symbolized by the use of a hot iron stamp to identify who owned the cattle. The concept of branding has certainly evolved from just branding cattle to a very viable business strategy that can help you stand out in a crowd. You definitely want to create your own brand as it sets you apart from your competition.

Branding Is a Personality

A brand is basically what a company stands for and what it is known for. In essence, a brand represents who that person or entity is, be it the quality of their product, the efficiency of their service, or their commitment to their customers. Ultimately, you want your brand to be something your customer can relate to or identify with. You want your brand to elicit a certain feeling or emotion that seemingly answers the question or solves the problem the customer may have.

Rob Frankel, a branding expert and author in Los Angeles, calls branding the most misunderstood concept in all of marketing, even among professionals. Branding, he says, "is not advertising and it's not marketing or PR. Branding happens before all of those: First you create the brand, then you raise awareness of it." Frankel continues to state that "branding is about getting your prospects to perceive you as the only solution to their problem. Once you're perceived as 'the only', there's no place else to shop. Which means your customers gladly pay a premium for your brand." (Klein 2012)

Your brand is your business identity. It is more than just your business name or the logo on your stationery and business cards. An effective brand tells your audience who you are, what you do and how you do it, while at the same time establishing your relevance to and credibility with your prospective customers. Your brand can establish the value of how your service or product is perceived by your audience. Perceived value, similar to perceived authority, is based on the image you portray through your brand. Please make note that there is a distinction between actual value and perceived value. The great thing, in relation to your brand, is that perceived value can be as powerful, if not more powerful, than actual value in many cases. Perceived value is determined by how the general public views and reacts to your brand. Brand perceptions are shaped by functional experiences (e.g., speed, detail, quality, reliability) as well as emotional experiences (e.g., makes me feel better, improves my knowledge and understanding, makes my real estate experience more gratifying or easier) that the customer associates with your service.

In relation, your brand must create a positive image in your customer's mind, as strong brands are memorable in the customer's heart and mind. Creating a positive brand value requires the building of trust, respect, and a mutual relationship with your customer. Your brand needs to be trusted that it will deliver the service that is promised in order to build the respect and the relationship you desire with your customer. An effective brand with a positive perceived value will communicate, engage and involve its customers in its value and benefits. In essence, you should have an open dialogue with your customer base and ask them about their expectations and whether or not your brand delivered on its promise.

Steps to Effective and Efficient Branding

- Identify what **product or service** you are going to brand.
- Define the **position** of your brand. Your brand needs to tell your audience who you are, what you do, and how you do it, while at the same time establishing your relevance to and credibility with your prospective customers.
- Identify what **promise** your brand makes. Creating a positive brand value requires the building of trust, respect, and a mutual relationship with your customer. Your brand needs to be trusted that it will deliver the service that is promised in order to build the respect and the relationship you desire.
- Determine how you will **present** your brand. How you present your brand (e.g., name, logo, sales presentations, ads, business cards, etc.) can make or break your ability to create and maintain customer interest and value. Your brand must create a positive image in your customer's mind, as strong brands are memorable in the customer's mind. Creating a positive brand value requires the building of trust, respect, and a mutual relationship with your customer.
- Be **consistent** in your branding efforts. This is probably where most agents come up short. Trust and respect are earned so it is imperative that you consistently communicate your brand position and promise to your target market.
- **Perception** is in the eye of the beholder. You have defined the position of your brand, identified the brand's promise, determined the brand's presence, and have been consistent in your branding efforts. The question now is: What is the audience's perception of your brand? Is your brand's perceived value a positive one?

By now, you should have come to the logical conclusion that you need to create your own brand. The question is: Where do you start?

Establishing Relevance and Credibility

As we stated earlier, your brand needs to tell your audience who you are, what you do, and how you do it, while at the same time establishing your relevance to and credibility with your prospective customers. With that said, your first step in the process of creating your own brand is to create a business summary. Your business summary will be an eye-opening exercise for you as you identify what your goals are, how you plan to accomplish those goals, and what actions—short term and long term—you are going to take to achieve those goals. A business summary is a condensed version of your overall business plan and should be approximately four or five pages. Your business summary should at least define your target market, specify your strengths and specialties (including your competitive advantages and anything else that sets you apart from your competition), lay out your time management requirements, identify who will be holding you accountable, and what your action plan will be. Your business summary will be your immediate "track to run on."

Branding as It Relates to Social Media

To understand blogging, you need to understand how brand (and authority) is integrated into your web presence while having a branded mind-set, especially within your Internet social network.

Right now, accept the fact that most of the people in your social network are not your friends. We say this because they don't know you from Adam. In many ways, when branding yourself or your business online, you have to think as if you were applying for a job and/or building your career. Typically, you should focus on your strengths, talents, experiences, and education. All the while you are building up your self-esteem and confidence to impact the type of clients you want to serve. In order to accomplish this, think of the following when creating a personal brand:

- Authority and brand position
- Competition
- Your mission
- Your abilities
- Your story
- Your guarantee
- Trustworthiness and honesty

Challenges with Social Media and Brand

The challenge with branding yourself through your social media network is that everything is public. Depending on your settings and profiles, you have little to no privacy. People can comment on any article, presentation, video, blog post, etc., and have the option of leaving positive feedback or sometimes, negative comments. Branding yourself through a social network is a production. You're on stage and you need to be at your best. So how do you be the best? Simply create quality content and have a systematic approach.

Systematize Your Personal Branding

Having a systematized approach with social networking can be one of the most rewarding and straightforward elements you can do to develop your individual and company brand. Recognize who you are and know how you want to tell the world your story. Make use of important social media platforms while linking everything back to your blog site. There is really only one trait that you need to have when blogging to your social network: *consistency*.

When using a system in social network, you create mind share. As long as you distribute quality and valuable information, consistently, to your network, you will have created a brand identity. Thus, your mission should be, anytime anybody thinks of real estate, they will think of me.

In Chapter 6, "How to Use Your Blog and Social Media Tools," we showed you how to create your own Internet marketing schedule to help you distribute content. Having a system in place will help you earn the trust and respect of your peers and clients.

8 | Being the Authority

Being the Best in Your Field

The best marketing position for most real estate agents is to be in a position that is "above" their competition. In other words, you want to position yourself as the best in the field (where "best" translates to "best results"). How do you achieve that positioning? You achieve that by establishing yourself as a leader and becoming an authority in your field, area (farm), and/or niche.

What Is an Authority?

Merriam-Webster defines authority, in part, as power to influence or command thought, opinion, or behavior. In essence, being an **authority** means to become a leader and an *expert in continuing to learn and educate yourself on your profession*. The first rule of being an expert is to acknowledge that it is a constant work in progress. All anyone can ever do is try to educate oneself on their profession with as little bias and agenda as possible.

Becoming the Authority

This chapter, and ultimately this book, will show you the steps, processes, and systems on how to create, build, and maintain your status as an authority within your real estate target market through power and influence of social media.

Becoming the leader or authority in your field will reward you with success whether it is money, fame, or personal satisfaction. You will find that real success does not come in the form of having the best blog content or SEO or social media awareness. All those are components that can help your success, no doubt about it, but if you want to be in the position where success comes to you—and it comes to you sustainably—building a loyal following that views you as the authority is second to none. Think about the people you believe to be an authority figure and you will find that when they speak, you listen. They tell you something's good, bad, or indifferent and you accept it without question. You accept their opinion, not because you don't have a mind of your own, but because they, in your mind, are an authority and have earned that trust and respect.

It is interesting to note that positions of authority may be earned *or* may be based solely on impression, perception, and/or a trained trait.

A Shocking Experiment

There was a newspaper ad saying the psychology department at Yale was running a little "experiment on memory," and paid volunteers were needed for the hour-long study.

Volunteer A arrives at the lab and meets two men—a research scientist in a lab coat and another volunteer, B. The research scientist proceeds to explain the study to both volunteers and tells the volunteers the study is about the effects of punishment on memory. The task of volunteer B will be to learn a series of word pairings (volunteer B is called the learner).

Volunteer A's task will be to test the learner's memory of the word pairs, and administer electric shocks for each wrong answer (volunteer A is called the teacher). And for every new wrong answer, the voltage goes up. The teacher is not sure about this whole thing, but it must be okay, right?

The testing begins, and when the learner misses a question, the teacher pulls a lever that delivers a mild shock. Over time, though, the shock levels increase, and the learner is grunting audibly. At 120 volts, he says the shocks are really starting to hurt. At 150 volts, he tries to quit. The research scientist tells the teacher to keep going, and that the shocks will cause no permanent tissue damage to the learner. The teacher continues questioning and delivering punishment for incorrect answers.

At 165 volts, the learner screams and at 300 volts, the learner refuses to respond any longer, as the shocks are impairing his mental capacities. The research scientist then tells the teacher to treat nonresponses as incorrect answers. The learner is screeching, kicking, and pleading for mercy with every subsequent shock, all the way up to 450 volts, when the research scientist finally stops the teacher.

An incredible story, but this couldn't possibly have really happened, right? Well, actually it did in 1963 at Yale, during a series of experiments by Stanley Milgram. (Milgram 1974) The Milgram experiment was quite interesting in that:

- Unbeknownst to the teacher, the learner was an actor.
- Unbeknownst to the teacher, there were no actual electric shocks given to the learner.
- Unbeknownst to the teacher, the study had **nothing** to do with memory.

What Milgram wanted to know was how far the teacher would go when told to continue to deliver those shocks, since the teacher thought the shocks were real. About two-thirds (65%) of the test subjects (teachers) administered every shock up to 450 volts, no matter how much the learner begged for mercy. However, when the research scientist *did not* encourage the test subjects to continue, the study found that the test subjects would have stopped giving punishment quite early on. Every aspect of the experiment had been carefully controlled to pull test subjects from a standard cross section of ages, occupations, and education levels.

A 2002 analysis of the original study confirmed the findings. What could possibly lead to this behavior? Milgram concluded it's our deep-seated sense of duty to authority. We are trained from childhood to respect and trust authority figures (such as scientists in lab coats), and the obedience that comes with it stays with us throughout our lives. In other words, they (the teachers) complied because the research scientist was perceived as authoritative and therefore, trustworthy.

Neuroscience reveals the somewhat frightening answer. Brain scans show that the decision-making parts of our brains often shut down when we encounter authoritative advice or direction. That's part of what makes authority so powerful and why authority carries great responsibility.

How is this study relevant to you as a real estate professional? This study reinforces the fact that people seek out and go to those individuals that they perceive to be one of authority and thus trustworthy. The bottom line is that once you create the impression of perceived authority, your real estate community/target market will respond to you as the "go-to" person that they can trust and respect for all their real estate questions and needs.

Establishing Yourself as an Authority

Establishing yourself as an authority in your community, area (farm), and/or niche (e.g., short sales, luxury homes, etc.) has obvious value. The question is how does one establish a position of authority within your chosen field? There are many ways to be an authority figure, but one stands out and is available to anyone if they have the proper mind-set, stay focused, and are consistent. That one way is the process of blogging! How does one go about doing this? Well, start by getting active, right away. Getting active right away means take action...create and implement a traditional (e.g., door knocking, cold-calling, mailings) and nontraditional (e.g., blogging, creating videos) plan that professionally and consistently reaches out to your target market. Please note if you are just getting started you are not going to influence anyone overnight. Authority requires seasoning, research, and/or experience in your field along with being able to present that experience in the right manner in front of your target audience.

You want your audience to come to you for advice and help. Once they start turning toward you for help, it means they are starting to look at you in a whole new different light. People in your community love the opportunity to be able to trust and rely on an authority figure, but they are not the only ones that love authority...Google does, as well...people respond to and follow important people more than others. In relation, Google ranks important pages and sites higher than others. (Clark 2012)

- We believed we could build a better search. We had a simple idea, that not all pages are created equal. Some are more important.
  - *Sergey Brin, Cofounder, Google*
- It's quite complicated and sounds circular, but we've worked out a way of calculating a website's importance.
  - *Larry Page, Cofounder, Google*
- To rank well, build a site so fantastic that it makes you an authority in your niche.
  - *Matt Cutts, Head of Google Web Spam Team*

The bottom line is that if people think you have authority, so will Google! How will Google and your audience find you to be an authority? Well, to become an authority and influence opinion, thought, and behavior in others online, you must create valuable content within your blog that others will want to read, follow and cite, or link to, in their online content. In addition to valuable content, write your blog in a personal manner as to encourage interaction through your blog dialogue, comments, and links back to your blog from other bloggers who are reading your blog. Capture your audience's attention by being passionate, open, and honest about your subject matter and promote your blog as often as possible to attract more readers.

The content and delivery of the blog you create will set the standard for your process of achieving authority status. Please make note that there is a distinction between actual authority and perceived authority. The great thing, in relation to blogging, is that perceived authority can be as powerful, if not more powerful, than actual authority in many cases. Perceived authority is determined by how the general public views you (via your content and delivery) as to whether you are the "expert" in the field *or* not. Again, if the general public thinks you're an authority, so will Google and the other search engines.

Whether you are a brand-new agent or have twenty years of real estate experience, your goal is to be perceived as the authority not only in your field, but specifically in your community. Let's assume you are an agent in downtown San Diego; your blogging would want to focus its content and delivery on the downtown community and specifically the high-rise buildings in the downtown area (assuming that is your farm area).

You may want to compare, contrast, and discuss the various units in the high-rises. Compare the units and relating amenities not only in the individual units (appliances, flooring, cabinetry, etc.), but also the community amenities such as the pool, tennis courts, etc. Does the building have elevators? If so, do the elevators go to the specific unit or to the floor with several units? How many parking spaces are included with the purchase? Most importantly your blogging should be bold, honest, and dare to point out the positives and negatives of the various buildings and/or units. This may not make you popular with your entire audience, but it will gain you respect with all that read your blog. Whether your audience likes you or not, if you are without bias and are honest and truthful, then you will gain respect, a greater audience, and eventually be viewed as an authority on the downtown San Diego marketplace!

Blogging and Authority

If authority means to become a leader and an *expert in learning your profession* by influencing or commanding thoughts, opinions, or behaviors, then what does it mean to have blogging authority?

Blogging technology and authority go hand in hand. If you are really working hard at getting found, organically, on the Internet you should not separate technology and authority. When marrying the two together you need to know the groom and bride of the ceremony.

What Is Blogging Authority?

Blogging authority means to become a leader and an expert by influencing individuals in both your blogging community as well as your social media network with the understanding that authority starts with your blog. Remember, your blog distributes influential information throughout your network.

Blogging authority is measured by:
- Topical Authority
- Incoming and Outgoing Authoritative Links
- Frequency of Content Distribution
- References from Other Sites

Topical Authority

Topical authority is content measured by categories; for example, business, gaming, legal, relationships, pets, self-improvement, real estate, automotive, etc. As you know by now, each of your blog posts can be categorized. However, just because your content is categorized, it's just as important to fully optimize your pages and post with appropriate metadata. For example, if you were to post an article in the category of Arts and Entertainment. Let's say that your article is called, "How to Clean Your Paintbrushes." Your categories, tags, and metadata would be as follows:

Category:	Arts and Entertainment
Subcategory:	Painting
Tags:	paint, solvent, brushes, paper, clean, oil paint, acrylic, art, paintbrushes, cleaning paintbrushes, oil paint, acrylic paint, paint dry, drying time, water helps
Title:	How to Clean Your Paintbrushes
Description:	Drying time and water helps when cleaning paint-brushes for oil paint, acrylic paint, or dry paint with any type of art.
Keywords:	paint, solvent, brushes, paper, clean, oil paint, acrylic, art, paintbrushes, cleaning paintbrushes, oil paint, acrylic paint, paint dry, drying time, water helps

This example above is fully optimized per the post page with a well-known category and subcategory. Thus, you have begun to build topical authority. Take it to the next level by applying authoritative links.

Authoritative Links

Using the example above, "How to Clean Your Paintbrushes," you might want to see what popular places on the web people visit online. We tried typing in painting. We received 614,000,000 results for painting. See Figure 8-1 below:

Search   About 614,000,000 results (0.12 se)

Figure 8-1. Search results for "painting."

Even more interesting are the top results that were returned, as shown in Figure 8-2:

painting

About 614,000,000 results (0.12 seconds)

Ad - Why this ad?

Painting Contractors - Quality Painting Services
www.rapaintingservices.com
3 Solutions in Just 1 Call

Painting - Wikipedia, the free encyclopedia
en.wikipedia.org/wiki/Painting
Painting is the practice of applying **paint**, pigment, color or other medium to a surface
(support base). The application of the medium is commonly applied to the ...
Oil painting - History of painting - Category:Painting techniques - Chinese
painting

Behr **Paint** and Wood Stain - House **Paint** and Wood Stains
www.behr.com/
Interior & Exterior Paints and Wood Stains - Need help with your home **painting**
project? Browse **paint** colors, search our extensive How-To **paint** guide library, ...

About.com **Painting** - Learn to Paint, Develop Art Skills with Free ...
painting.about.com/
1 hour ago - Learn to **paint** and express your creativity under the guidance of an
experienced artist. Whether you're into **painting** with oils, acrylics, ...
Free Stencils Collection - Painting With Acrylics - Oil Painting Techniques -
Pastels

Figure 8-2. Top search results for "painting."

Besides the search result of the advertiser, the top three results were:

- Wikipedia
- Behr
- About.com

All three are well-known sources that relate to painting. They have built tremendous authority online and offline. Making a link to them would be a smart and strategic move on your part. It could be as simple as referencing the different types of colors on Behr.com or the different types of elements there are in painting being linked to Wikipedia. A link to these credible and trusted resources builds on your blogging authority just by referencing the sites that have influence on those who are interested in painting.

Frequency of Content Distribution

Time frame in blogging is important when building influential authority. Leadership and expertise do not come overnight. It's built on honesty, competency, inspiration, reputation, etc. This is why it is important to have the right mind-set when you start blogging.

Consistency and following an Internet marketing schedule marked in your calendar is important when distributing posts, guides, e-books, presentations, and more. After six months of consistent distribution of quality post to your network, you should start to see results in viewership, e-mails, and phone calls. This is so because you have spent your time in truly helping the industry that you are targeting. And, this is what the search engines are looking for; they want consistent posts by your blogging machine.

Referenced from Other Blogs

This is fairly simple. Get other sites to reference you and hyperlink back to your blog. You can also be more proactive by commenting on an article by making a remark on another blog site. If blog owner accepts your comment, then a link will go back to your site.

Figure 8-3. An example of commenting on another blog site.

Search engines will recognize where a site is being linked from, which gives you more authority. You can also view this in your blog dashboard. See an example of a comment on another site in Figure 8-3.

Now there is interaction. The names in the example are hyperlinked, linking back to Darren Tunstall's real estate blog. Consider making comments on other blog sites.

Another Type of Search Engine: Technorati

Did you know that there are different types of search engines? For example, we have all heard of Google, Yahoo!, and Bing, right? But have you heard of Technorati?

Most people have never heard of this company, but it is sensitive to your blogging efforts. Technorati indexes a million-plus blogs. They are the basis for top stories, views, pictures, and videos rising across news broadcasts, entertainment, technology, lifestyle, sports, government, and business.

Technorati is also known as being the most inclusive and up-to-date company of who and what is admired in the blogging community. For this reason, it is important that you get familiar with Technorati. They can be found at http://www.technorati.com. Once you are at the Technorati site, do the following:

- Join (if new) or sign in.
- Develop your profile and bio.
- Add your image.
- Claim your blog.

When claiming your blog, follow the instructions provided by Technorati. They are very clear and simple to follow. Once Technorati approves your site, they will start indexing your postings. Search engines use this data to help build your online authority.

The industry is constantly changing. Technorati will help you stay informed, as they are the authority in this field.

As we mentioned earlier in this chapter, becoming the leader or authority in your field will reward you with success, whether it is money, fame, or personal satisfaction. Without question, the goal of becoming the leader or authority is obtained by building a loyal following that views you as the authority. You will create a loyal following by providing your audience with excellent content and delivering that content to your audience on a consistent basis.

9 | Lead Generation

What Is Lead Generation?

Wikipedia defines lead generation as follows: "Lead generation is a marketing term used, often in Internet marketing, to describe the generation of consumer interest or inquiry into products or services of a business. Leads can be generated for a variety of purposes; for example: list building, e-newsletter list acquisition, or for winning customers."

Methods for Generating Leads

There are many tactical methods for generating leads. These methods typically fall under the umbrella of advertising, but may also include:

- Nonpaid sources such as organic search engine results.
- Referrals from existing customers.

Businesses strive to generate "quality" leads. Quality is usually determined by the propensity of the inquirer to take the next action towards a purchase.

Wikipedia notes that lead generation is particularly used in Internet marketing. The truth is that lead generation is used in many aspects well beyond Internet marketing. If you really think about it, most, if not all, businesses and professionals lead generate in one form or fashion, whether they realize it or not. Lead generation is much more than just Internet marketing or acquiring a list of names and then cold-calling, door knocking, placing ads, or mailing. Lead generation is absolutely necessary and critical to building and sustaining a successful business practice. With the advent of new technology, there are new lead-generating opportunities, which are much more sophisticated and in some terms more efficient and effective (e.g., blogging).

Results-Oriented Lead Generation

Results-oriented lead generation is an art or, at the very least, an acquired skill. There are many facets that come into play to get the results you want to achieve with your lead generation system. However, before we can discuss your lead generation system, there are several powerful components that need to be identified, developed, and maintained as a foundation to building your successful lead generation system. These powerful components include:

- Creating your **business summary**
- Forming a **positive mind-set**
- Instilling a crystal clear **focus**
- Establishing a specific daily **time management** format
- Taking **action**
- Being held **accountable** for each of these components

Let's briefly review these powerful components:

Business Summary

A **business summary** is the first thing you want to complete in this process. Your business summary is a condensed written version of your overall business plan and should be approximately four or five pages. As mentioned in Chapter 7, your business summary should at least define your target market, specify your strengths and specialties (including your competitive advantages and anything else that sets you apart from your competition), lay out your time management requirements, identify who will be holding you accountable, and what your action plan will be.

Positive Mind-Set

What is a **positive mind-set**? When one has a positive mind-set, they think and feel in a positive way and typically envision happiness, good health, success, and perceive a positive outcome to just about every situation and event that takes place. They also trust that they will make the right decision and the right choices in most instances. Since they expect it—their conscious mind and subconscious mind will find a way to make it happen. This is the power of having a positive mind-set. Thus, to form a positive mind-set you have to develop a positive thinking pattern and you have to realize that positive thinking is not something you do randomly. Positive thinking is a practice, one that you will have to work with daily and apply regularly. By making positive thinking a daily habit you create a positive mind-set that allows you to avoid potentially negative and challenging situations, and helps you resolve challenges quickly and easily. With a positive mind-set in place you will naturally enjoy a better, more focused, and rewarding business and lifestyle.

Focus

Merriam-Webster's dictionary defines **focus** as a state or condition permitting clear perception or understanding. We have found that in business and, more specifically, in real estate blogging that agents may initially have the focus but quickly lose that focus over time. Focus and staying consistent with your blogging effort is extremely important in achieving results in your lead generation. Lack of focus is most often the number one reason real estate agents do not achieve results through their blogging efforts. As Tony Robbins stated,

> "One reason so few of us achieve what we truly want is that we never direct our focus; we never concentrate our power.

Most people dabble their way through life, never deciding to master anything in particular." (Robbins 1991, 21)

Time Management

Time management and focus go hand in hand, as you will require focus to stay consistent and on track with your control over the amount of time spent on specific activities in relation to your daily activities. Time blocking, an important aspect to time management, is the daily function of literally planning out your day's activities on an hour-by-hour basis. For example, a managing broker may block:

- 8:00 a.m. to 9:00 a.m. for agent communication (respond to e-mails, listen to voicemail, individual agent meeting)
- 9:00 a.m. to 11:00 a.m. for lead generation (recruiting outside agents)
- 11:00 a.m. to 12:00 p.m. for office administration
- 12:00 p.m. to 12:30 p.m. for lunch
- 12:30 p.m. to 2:00 p.m. for office business (review transactions, insurance, accounting, etc.)
- 2:00 p.m. to 4:00 p.m. for agent recruit meetings and/or lead generation
- 4:00 p.m. to 5:30 p.m. for agent retention and communication, office admin, and "other"

Time blocking is essential to effective time management and must strictly be followed. Do not let distractions pull you off your scheduled activities. Stay focused on your task at hand! As an exercise, list your activities that you did yesterday in a time blocked fashion (e.g., what you did from 8:00 a.m. to 9:00 a.m.; from 9:00 a.m. to 10:00 a.m., etc.) and be honest, now! If you find that you were all over the place, you can make more effective use of your time with a little planning. Now, in preparation for tomorrow, time block your activities on an hourly basis and we are confident that not only will you be much more efficient in your time and activities, but you will find that you end up with a lot more time at the end of the day that you can spend on yourself!

Action

In relation to taking **action**, you want to take any type of action toward achieving the task and/or goal that you set out for yourself that day, week, month, etc. It really is that simple, but you would be amazed as to how many agents are just too busy preparing to take action, but never actually do anything! As we stated earlier in the book, get going right away and take action...create and implement a traditional (e.g., door knocking, cold-calling, mailings) and nontraditional (e.g., blogging, videos, presentations, e-books, etc.) plan that professionally and consistently reach out to your target market.

Accountability

Accountability is a mutually engaging process that you partake in with someone you respect and is centered on your continuous focus and refocus. It is difficult to set hard goals and then stay consistent and devoted to achieving those goals on your own. The benefit to this process is that you hold each other accountable to the goals and aspirations that you each want to achieve. Many top achievers have accountability partners or coaches that keep them motivated and on track. Daily, weekly, and/or monthly goals are set and discussed and you are then held accountable to achieve those goals as you communicate with your accountability partner on a regular basis. Accountability is all about consistently getting and using feedback to keep you focused and on track to achieve your goals. My accountability partner is my coauthor! I trust and respect his opinion and we set goals, assign tasks, and communicate on a continuous basis. We know that we are each hard workers and that we do not want to let the other down, which is a great motivator for getting up and making sure the tasks get done within the time frame that we set for one another.

What Is the Lead Generation Process?

Now that we know the powerful components that set up the foundation for a results-oriented lead generation system, what is the lead generation process all about? First of all, refer to your business summary to identify your target market, type of leads you are looking for, your budget (blogging is very inexpensive, but you may be looking at leads from other sources), and the amount of time on a daily basis that you are going to devote to lead generation.

There are many forms and styles of the lead generation process and we certainly recommend that you have several forms of lead generation in your business plan that you use on a consistent basis. With that said, some forms of lead generation can be more efficient and effective than others. The "traditional" types of lead generation have typically included:

- Cold-calling
- Door knocking
- E-mail blasts
- Trade shows
- Outsourced telemarketing
- Advertising

Traditional real estate lead generation *reaches out to people with the hope that they might be interested* in buying or selling a property. The advent of technology has brought a new dimension to lead generation. Technology and social media have personalized the process of lead generation by providing an *avenue for people to find and get to "know" you on a personal and business level* by just connecting to you via the Internet. It soon becomes obvious that your name, authority (actual or perceived), and brand are extremely beneficial in the lead generation process simply because men and women like to do business with those they "know," like, and trust. This new dimension of lead generation, if done properly, is very efficient, results-oriented, and is extremely inexpensive.

Some say that the lead generation process is all about generating revenue. Actually, creating revenue is the by-product of the lead generating process. When carefully analyzed, the lead generating process is simply about setting appointments to make listing presentations to sellers and buyers. Thus, the process of lead generation is to get the lead, then convert the lead to an appointment, then convert the appointment to a listing, then sell the listing and generate revenue for you.

Now that we know the powerful components that set up the foundation for a results-oriented lead generation system and what is the lead generation process all about, what are the essentials to make our blogs the most effective lead generators?

Essentials to Capturing Leads

Any type of user can find your blog on the search engines, but the trick is to target those who need your products and services. Here are a few things you can do to capture targeted leads:

- Be consistent by writing in your blog using the Internet marketing schedule (IMS).
- Provide a variety of content as suggested in Chapter 6.
- Optimize your post and pages with popular keywords, tags, and categories as described in Chapter 5.
- Provide users with clear calls to action by giving them options to want to give you their name, phone number, and e-mail. Some examples are to opt in for an e-book, sign up for a webinar, or to provide and e-mail for downloading a presentation.
- Build authoritative hyperlinks that are related to the post in an effort to build credibility with the search engines while encouraging backlinks.

10 | Relationship Marketing Strategy

Relationship marketing is a strategy that is focused on developing strong connections with customers by providing them with valuable information specifically designed to fit their needs and interests. Customers will always do business with people they know, like, and trust. That's the essence of relationship marketing. Basically, relationship marketing means that you put people first, before the money, before the fancy website and all the bells and whistles. Relationship marketing is based on creating a mutually beneficial exchange between you and your customers and/or potential customers.

Relationships begin when you get to know your customers on a personal level and you let them get to know you. In essence, it's about creating value and developing trust in each other. When you provide product and service that customers value, they are motivated to relate more with you and your brand. Relationships that build and get stronger over time lead to greater revenue and higher profits for you. As these relationships grow, you will find that your customer's behavior becomes completely predictable and controllable, which will make your marketing efforts more effective and easier.

There is definitely a strategy to effective relationship marketing and it centers on consistent personal and open communication with your customer base over time. A successful relationship marketing strategy involves developing a close relationship with your audience. To a great extent, that means providing valuable content for them that will help them solve their problems, answer their questions, and/or provide solutions/education for situations they may be experiencing. Social media and your blogs are excellent opportunities to provide such support, but don't stop there. Your blogs (and your other online and offline forms of marketing and lead generation) should allow your audience the opportunity to get to personally know you so they can begin the process of trusting and respecting you. People get tired of hearing just the business side of someone, so share information and stories about yourself (a little about your family, what you like to do when you are not working, your pets, etc.) so people can get to know who you are and where you are coming from.

The goal of relationship marketing is to build customer loyalty and their commitment to you and your brand. A successful relationship marketing strategy will ultimately focus on customer retention, which will result in higher levels of new business and repeat business for you. It is logical to assume that loyal customers will be repeat customers and that will certainly be more profitable for you. Again, it's not about the money, it's about taking care of your customers and, simply, getting them to like you and trust you. Your customers will appreciate your caring and will not only buy from you time and time again, but also recommend you to others. The money will follow and loyal customers are usually more willing to pay more for your brand of product or service. Loyal customers are also less costly to serve and typically give positive word-of-mouth advertising for you, your brand, and/or service.

Traditional marketing in the past consisted primarily of ad print and radio and television ads to sell products and services. Although the traditional style of marketing is still widely used, it typically does not connect with consumers on a personal and emotional level. With that said, it is important to recognize that the ever-increasing popularity of Internet resources, specifically social media, is providing the opportunity for people to identify with their target market and openly communicate with that target market in an interactive way to connect with their audience on a personal and emotional level. This connection creates relationships with the consumer and that ultimately translates into sales.

Relationship marketing is an effective strategy that engages and encourages your customers to interact with you and your brand. It provides an interesting interaction between unique product/service information and your customer's lifestyle, education, support, desires, and demands. Relationship marketing provides all this in a relevant and customer-friendly approach. In relation, please make note of the following suggestions:

- **Know your customer:** research, analyze, and understand your customer's needs, and then develop a plan that will build knowledge, confidence, and motivation.
- **Allow your customer to get to know you:** be open, purposeful, and genuine in your communications with your customers.
- **Listen to your customer:** encourage dialogue through surveys, member feedback, market research, and social media, engaging your customers in the process and gaining deeper insight into their needs.
- **Develop your marketing plan:** identify those customers who are most likely to take the desired action and target your plan and communication accordingly. This will maximize the effectiveness of your plan and will ultimately result in sales.
- **Provide multiple ways for customer interaction:** give consumers a variety of ways in which to communicate with you and your brand, maximizing the plan's effectiveness and value.
- **Focus on excellent customer service:** make excellent customer service the number-one goal by providing information and support at every point of contact.

- **Create accountability:** integrate a form of measurement into every level of the plan so that the various levels of your plan can be identified and measured for results and effectiveness and then modified, if need be.

As we mentioned, relationship marketing centers on getting to know your customers. Who they are and how they act gives you the knowledge to make marketing, sales, or customer service decisions. When applied strategically and consistently over time, your relationship marketing plan will create a strong bond between your brand and your customers; a relationship so strong that your customers will continue to stay and remain loyal to you and your brand for the long term.

Many successful companies such as Nordstrom, Walmart, and Starbucks have invested their time, energy, money, and reputation on relationship marketing. Walmart, an extremely large and successful retailer, is an excellent example of the simple power of relationship marketing. Walmart places a greeter at the entrance/exit doors to their stores with the sole purpose of showing their customers that they are appreciated. The greeter thanks the customers for coming in, assists them with a shopping cart, and with a smile says thank you and good-bye as the customer leaves the store. The greeter is typically a senior citizen dressed in a blue vest that genuinely exudes a warm and friendly personality to every customer coming in or out of a Walmart store.

Relationship Marketing Is a Commitment

Relationship Marketing is a commitment to customer service and just making your customer feel good. Your relationship marketing strategy should focus, as did Walmart's, on the following elements:

- Your marketing has to be **personalized**. The Walmart greeter's smile and thank you worked very well in personalizing the relationship. Personalization is effective in the traditional form of a specifically targeted direct mail piece, a phone call, or an e-mail. Equally, if not more, effective is the use of social media and the art of systematic and continuous blogging.

- Your marketing has to be **targeted**. Walmart invests money in maintaining relationships by creating value with existing customers. By targeting this group, Walmart establishes long-term relationships with their "regular" shoppers. Targeting these customers through programs that reward loyalty can result in an excellent return on investment over the life of the customer.

- Your marketing has to be **meaningful**. Your marketing plan has to connect in an emotional way to establish a lasting relationship. The message that you want to convey must be genuine, informative, and of value to your customer. If the Walmart greeter were not genuine in his greeting and smile, the greeting would not have a lasting impact with the customer.

- Your marketing should be **interactive**. Interestingly, many Walmart greeters learn the names of the frequent shoppers and greet them accordingly. It is important to make relationship marketing interactive so you can hear feedback, then determine what is working and what is not. Blogging is an outstanding source for interaction with your customers. Blogging gives you the opportunity to communicate with your customers, provide the most current news or information, offer special online deals and, equally important, your customer can immediately communicate with you.

These are essential elements necessary for a successful relationship marketing strategy. The key for you is to integrate these elements into your daily blogs. Logically speaking, consistent blogging is relationship marketing at its best. There are many factors that make blogging an extremely powerful marketing tool, such as personal interaction through comments, instant notification of page updates through RSS feeds, and the overall friendly personalized tone and writing of the blog posts themselves. Coupled with the proven high search engine optimization value of blogs, they are an opportunity to maximize the value of your relationship marketing strategy. As you blog, and as this book illustrates, you will provide helpful information, education, and links to other sites that will benefit your audience. Your audience will then have the opportunity to communicate with you and other audience members to ask questions, give comments, and even provide additional information and links. This is the essence of relationship marketing and your audience will not only begin to trust and follow you, but will be motivated to use and recommend your services.

11 | Insider Tips

Get Active, Socially

You absolutely have to get active, socially, in front of your field and related community. If you want to be viewed as an authority in your industry, you must engage with your audience on social community sites like Facebook, Twitter, YouTube, blogs, etc. You also want to make your website a destination that promotes to and from interaction.

Teach People, Don't Sell Them

In general, people want to buy, not be sold to. Although, you need people to complete your forms so that you can capture them as leads, you do this by offering free useful and valuable information that helps them, something that tells them to listen to you because you are the expert.

Content Arsenal

Content is the reason why people visit your site. Through your content, you have created an awareness of your expertise and leadership. Having valuable content readily available will help potential prospects determine if they want to do business with you. Not only is content what learners are looking for, but it's also what search engines are looking for, too. Remember to use the different types of content that we discussed in Chapter 6 under "Building a Content Factory."

Getting Your Blog Read

To begin, you need to read Chapter 1, "Getting Started," and Chapter 6, "How to Use Your Blog and Social Media Tools." These will give you a good idea of what tools you should be using, especially when optimizing your post pages for SEO. You should also read the chapters on relationships, branding, and authority so that you can understand why you are doing what we ask of you.

Tips That Work

- **Pictures.** They tell a thousand words. The most obvious is pictures of homes. In fact, according to NAR, 85% of home buyers found property photos to be the most useful online (NAR 2010). You can also post pictures that encourage conversation. For example:

Figure 11-1. Example of a sign that is a conversation starter.

- **Questions.** For example, "Dentist cures cancer?" This could lead into an article discussing the possibility of a dentist curing cancer. You want to pique the interest of the reader.

- **Visual organization.** Break up your articles/post in paragraphs using heading titles such H1, H2, and H3 tags. Use bullet points, numbers, **bold**, *italics*, etc. These help the reader navigate through your content. Web users scan. Typically, they don't read. So make it easy for them.

- **Odd numbers.** People like odd numbers. For example, "Man pays $14,564 for home." It makes us want to take a second look. Don't just make stuff up, though. Use real facts that you can back up.

- **Percentages.** "95% of home buyers and sellers are going to the Internet before ever talking to a real estate agent." Whether you agree or not, it's interesting. Think about the polls with candidates running for president. We love those numbers, don't we? And we even argue with ourselves if our candidate is not ahead.

- **Don't finish your post.** This is a technique that you can use to gain more interest. People want to know the end of the story. They might even e-mail you to ask what your point was. NOTE: even though it is not finished, you should still optimize it with good keywords and metadata while tagging and categorizing.

- **Videos.** For example, [Video]—Buying Real Estate on Mars. Rather than read, people like to be told what to do. Think about audio books. Use brackets in your subject to tell people what is included.

- **Free reports.** Use free reports to get your readers to opt in. Once they do, put them on a systematic drip campaign telling them about your products or services. We suggest you write your own content. That way it will be unique. In this case, you could provide an e-book as discussed in Chapter 6 under Phase 3: High-Touch Preparation and Low-Touch Circulation.

- **Curiosity, confusion, and shock**. People love to gossip. Think about this example, "Donald Trump retires?" or "Why I love strip clubs." How about this one, "Dummy sentenced 15 years for selling seats?"

- **Claim your blog on Technorati.** This is a gold nugget we're giving to you right now. All you have to do is go there and learn. Follow the step-by-step instructions that we laid out for you in Chapter 8 under the section "Another Type of Search Engine: Technorati."

- **Negative subject lines.** Be careful with this one. You don't want to turn people away. This is used to create curiosity. An example could be, "SUBJ: Brushing your teeth sucks... (maybe)," or "SUBJ: I hate the law and the law won," and "SUBJ: Five words...what's in it for me?"

- **Useful information.** This is obvious, but it's just something we have to say. Provide valuable information that your readers can use, period. For example, we wrote a post called "What Is a Notice of Default?"

What Is A Notice of Default

Posted on January 20, 2012 by admin

Question

I missed payments on my mortgage due to medical bills. I checked into short selling my home in San Diego, but I never did follow through. Now, I have a notice of default claiming that if I don't catch up, then a notice of trustee sale will be enforced, putting my house in San Diego up for auction. What is a notice of default?

Figure 11-2. A post offering valuable information.

In the example above, we also gave an answer in text along with a video answer placed on YouTube. The result was many phone calls generated from this one posting alone. Some of which were out of state.

- **Alternate post types.** See Chapter 6 for content recommendations when building a content factory. For example, on Mondays feature something in your industry like a property for sale, type of insurance policy, new brushing techniques, etc. On Tuesdays write an article reporting the news. On Wednesdays editorialize an article that you read and give your opinion (hyperlink to the article). On Thursday, create a short video. You get the point. Don't just give the same information everyday otherwise; people will see the giant pink elephant.

- **Rewrite your permalink structure.** Although we talked about this in the chapter on setting up your blog, we want to remind you to actually do it. You want the titles of your pages and post to be part of your URL simply because with a custom permalink, the search engines can read your title as if it were a sentence and not a run-on sentence.

- **Don't force people to register.** If you create valuable information that people can use and establish yourself as the authority, people will complete your forms. If you force junk on them, they know, and they will not fill out your forms.

- **Comment on your own post.** Sounds a little crazy, but it can help encourage conversation. We just need to help your viewers get started.

- **Consistency.** We put this last on our list because we want you to know that consistency is the key to having a successful blog. If you stop, visitors will stop because search engines don't have new content from your blog site to serve. Consequently, leads will decrease.

There are many more tips and tricks to share with you and we certainly have enjoyed sharing our time-tested strategies. As we continue to experiment with this powerful but fast-changing online environment, we will be sharing even more techniques online at http://greleads.com.

12 | **IDX for MLS and Real Estate**

What Is IDX?

IDX means Internet data exchange, frequently called broker reciprocity. As another phase within the development of the MLS, IDX is definitely the prime means of improving cohesiveness between real estate agents and brokers to facilitate purchasing and sale of property. IDX allows MLS members the application they need to showcase each other's listings on their Internet blog sites. Inside of the IDX real estate system, companies exchange approval to display one another's listings on the web. With IDX you can have maximum control of which property listings you actually present. As a result, IDX is the one of best pieces of content that you can present to buyers and sellers.

Why Use IDX?

One of the biggest reasons why you should use IDX is because it allows you to acquire and retain original communication with visitors to your site and all through the real estate transaction. This is important as it relates to lead generation and referrals. If you do a good job during your initial contact with clients, then you can go back and ask for friends and family contact information. Now, you've turned your first-time visitor to a satisfied client who is willing to share more names and numbers with you. Thus, IDX has allowed you to take lead generation to a second level of referral clients, offline. We say offline as a reminder that in referral situations, you need to practice traditional, proven sales methods by using the phone, sending postcards, dropping by to say hello, etc.

Advantages and Features of IDX

There are so many advantages to having an IDX integrated into your blog site that it is almost impossible to list all of them in this one chapter. We could write a whole book on just IDX. To get the gist of what an IDX does, we have handpicked several features that we feel will be the most beneficial to you and your blog visitors.

Blog Site Integration

Integration of an IDX is extremely easy through the use of plug-ins. You just need to know which plug-in is the best. There are many, and of course, we have our preference; you need to choose which company meets your blogging style and Internet marketing schedule. Some integration features include:
- IDX details inserted into pages and posts
- Live listings current with MLS
- URLs with custom search capability
- City pages generated automatically
- Neighborhood pages generated automatically
- Google Maps with search results
- Content combination according to MLS data
- Auto sitemaps for search engines

Property Facts

Home sellers and especially buyers are looking for details. They want the factual information that is valuable so that they can make a decision to either call or e-mail you about a particular property. If you are posting content on your blog site regularly (with IDX, you can create a unique post of a property in less than five minutes) and have your social media set up properly, people will find the information in one of two ways:

1. They will see it on their social media sites such as Facebook and Twitter.
2. They will find it via searching on search engines including Google, Yahoo!, and Bing.

Some property details include:
- A history of the home's sale price.
- A slideshow of the home's photos with a full-size photo viewer.
- School district information (this is important because generally people want their kids to go to a good school).
- Forms to contact you about a particular property (when it comes to you it references the property and MLS number they are interested in).
- Branding, with your name and number on a PDF flyer (this is huge for creating quick presentations). We feature at least one property every day and send it through our social network.
- Walkability ratings, and maps that include a bird's-eye view of where the property is located in a given area (provided by major search engines).

Advance Customization

Customization allows you to develop a system according to how you feel your visitors will interact with your blog site. As you move along in your online efforts, you will begin to study the analytical reasons of what, when, where, and how people are interacting on your site in an effort to determine the "why." For example, if you find that people are visiting your site by typing into the search engines using MLS numbers versus addresses, then you might want to give visitors the option on your home page (or every page) the ability to type in MLS numbers. In the example below in Figure 12-1, we have included the space for people to type in the actual MLS number indicated by MLS #:

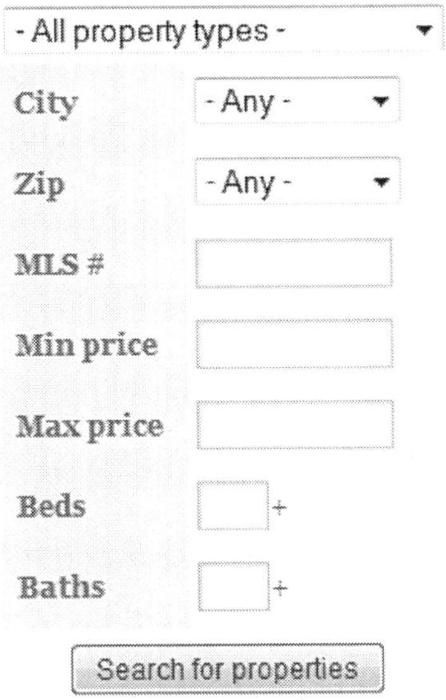

- All property types -   ▼

City   - Any -   ▼

Zip   - Any -   ▼

MLS #   [   ]

Min price   [   ]

Max price   [   ]

Beds   [   ] +

Baths   [   ] +

[Search for properties]

Figure 12-1. An example of a customized search box including MLS#.

Analytics allows you to study this information and it is your job to go back to your IDX to customize how people are able to interact. Some advance custom features include:

- Sorting of properties by different variables including time, price, size, etc.
- Custom pages titles. In another chapter we discuss permalinks and having you URLs reflect what your page or post is titled. For example, a listing available on the IDX with an address of 1234 Name of Street in San Diego, CA 90000. The IDX would display as: http://yourdomain.com/idx/mls-123456789-1234_ name_of_st_san_diego_ca_90000. This is important because search engines look at the URL and see spaces or sentences, indicated by an underscore (_) or a dash/hyphen (-). The search engines can read this as a grammatically correct sentence.
- Specify layout of city, neighborhood, and listing pages.

- Allow short sale and foreclosure search.
- Allow address or MLS number searching.
- Office or Agent ID (meaning if you want to dedicate a page just to your listings or your office).

Integrate with Other Online Systems

With the right IDX provider, you can integrate features that will help you and your visitors in several ways:

1. Allowing visitors to interact and share your blogs listings via e-mail, Twitter, Facebook, etc.
2. Let visitors comment on properties or locations such as cities, communities, or even particular zip codes.
3. Search engine results via the sitmap.xml for all major search engines including Google, Yahoo!, and Bing

You can also integrate walk scores, which calculate the walkability of an address based on its surroundings in any city or neighborhood. This way, you can see what is nearby. A walk score is another valuable piece of information to give your visitors; they can determine whether they want to live in that area or not based on its surroundings. Figure 12-2 shows an example of a walk score rating:

Property Type(s): Residential / Detached, Residential / All

Last Updated	2/14/2012	Tract	Bonita
Year Built	1968	Community	Bonita
County	San Diego	Walk Score ®	26 ?

Figure 12-2. Example of a walk score rating.

The lower the walk score number, the less walkability the property has. Meaning, the more the home owner will need to drive. Once a visitor clicks on the score they will be presented with more details such as nearby restaurants, grocery stores, parks, banks, etc. The property will also be visible on a map to give a more visual perspective. See Figure 12-3:

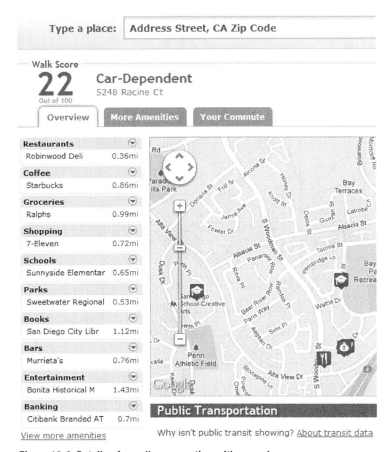

Figure 12-3. Details of a walk score rating with map view.

In the example above, the home is not even displayed. It typically is displayed with an icon of a house, see arrow below in Figure 12-4:

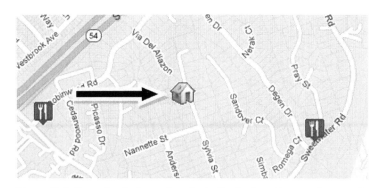

Figure 12-4. Example of a house icon typically displayed in map view results.

This is a good indicator that a resident might have to drive everywhere in their neighborhood. As you can see, walk scores are valuable and buyers use them to help make purchasing decisions. When selling a home, you can use them to your advantage by pulling out the places nearby and using as part of a marketing presentation to buyers or buyers agents.

Compliance, Support, and Dependability

If you are considering IDX for your blog, then search for an IDX provider who offers good support by phone, e-mail, and/or live chat. You can also join in on webinars and participate in support forums and recorded videos.

Finally, IDX companies are under strict review by National Association of Realtors and local MLS boards. NAR and local MLS providers make guidelines available and it is the IDX company's responsibility to make sure they are current on everything with national and local rules. Good IDX providers keep their systems up-to-date and pass this along to blogs, seamlessly, on each page and post that uses their tools. This allows you to be in full compliance with your local MLS board and NAR. This is a priority in an IDX search.

Having an IDX is great tool to have on your blog. We also like to think of it as having unlimited content for your visitors and prospective buyers and sellers. After all, if you are a real estate agent, part of your job is to present properties. IDX will help you do this while providing excellent, valuable and useful information to search engines, authority sites, and of course home buyers and sellers. We are constantly seeking out companies who provide the best product with good customer support. In doing this, if you find yourself saying, *I need IDX*, then know that we keep track of IDX providers at http://greleads.com. We also have our favorite IDX provider listed in the appendix.

We hope you consider incorporating an IDX into your blog for your visitors.

A | Appendix

Index for Online Social Media Marketing Channels of Distribution (SMMCD)

The best way for us to explain social media marketing channels of distribution (SMMCD) is that of a manufacturer and raw materials. In manufacturing, raw materials are the basic materials from which a product is manufactured. For example, in making paper, the raw materials used are:

- Wood
- Fiber from sawmills
- Recycled newspaper
- Vegetable matter
- Recycled cloth
- Chemicals

The raw materials above for making paper are just the basics and can be considered as categories for raw materials in making paper. There are subcategories, too, such as what type of trees for the wood, types of fiber from the sawmills, and vegetable plants such as bamboo, sugarcane, and flax. Chemical raw materials used in paper manufacturing include bleaches and dyes to change colors, break down other raw materials, etc. You get the point!

Using raw materials on the Internet to market your business is no different than making paper offline for people to write on.

Everything listed below is a raw material for creating an online presence. The question is if you are willing to use these raw materials to create the product, brand, authority, and Internet presence that you want in an effort to generate valuable and useful information to attract leads.

All the materials below get plugged into the manufacturing system (your blog), and then get circulated (via Twitter, FeedBurner, Ping.fm, etc.) to retailers, customers, and/or end users.

Articles (Syndicated News)

Ask.com – http://www.ask.com

Ask.com is the #1 question answering service that delivers the best answers from the web and real people—all in one place.

Bing.com – http://www.bing.com

Bing is a search engine that finds and organizes the answers you need so you can make faster, more informed decisions.

Blogs – Other People's Blogs (OPB)

Other people's blogs give you a prospective of what others are thinking, as well as allows for you to comment with your own opinions.

Google – http://www.google.com

Search the world's information, including web pages, images, videos, and more.

Yahoo! – http://www.yahoo.com

Quickly find what you're searching for, get in touch with friends, and stay in the know.

Article Directory

Articlesbase – http://www.articlesbase.com

Find free online articles for your website, blog, newsletters, etc.

Article Dashboard – http://www.articledashboard.com

Submit articles to the Article Dashboard directory, search and find free website and Ezine content, and open an author submission management account.

Ezine Articles – http://Ezinearticles.com

Ezine Articles allows expert authors in hundreds of niche fields to get massive levels of exposure in exchange for the submission of their quality original articles.

YellowBrix – http://www.yellowbrix.com

Provider of syndicated news content for portals and intranets.

Squidoo – http://www.squidoo.com

A popular, free site for creating single web pages on your interests and recommendations.

Audio

iTunes – http://www.itunes.com

Upload your own music, movies, TV shows, etc., to iTunes in the Cloud for others to review.

Podcast – http://en.wikipedia.org/wiki/Podcast

A podcast is a type of digital media format consisting of periodic sequence of collections, video or audio, subscribed to and downloaded through online syndication.

Blogs

RSS Feeds – http://www.feedzilla.com/

RSS feeds benefit publishers by letting them syndicate content automatically. You can also go to feed providers such as Feedzilla and search for RSS Feeds. You can add freshness to your blog and brand yourself as an expert.

Ping-0-Matic – http://pingomatic.com/

Updates multiple services and search engines about updates to weblog content with a single ping.

Trackbacks – http://en.wikipedia.org/wiki/Trackback

A trackback is one of three types of linkback methods for web authors to request notification when somebody links to one of their documents. Visit your tutorial section of your blog platform to learn how to include trackbacks on your site. Examples of current users of trackbacks include WordPress, Drupal, Joomla, and Movable Type.

Commenting

This is where you can read Other People's Blogs (OPB) and comment on their post. Use the search engines to find available blog sites that allow commenting.

Guest Posting

Guest posting allows readers of your blog post to share your post with their social networks, building you more links and allowing you to grow your authority, reputation, and brand. Sites that readers usually use are Twitter, Digg, Facebook, and StumbleUpon.

Blog Hosting and Domain Name Tools

iAgentc – http://www.iagentc.com

Offers full service online resource tools for professionals and small businesses with domain names, website, blogs, hosting, email, SEO, analytics and more to attract home buyer leads, home seller leads and real estate investors.

iAgentc.com

E-books and Reports

Scribd – http://www.scribd.com

Scribd is a social publishing site, where tens of millions of people share original writings and documents. Scribd's vision is to liberate the written word.

Scribd.

Amazon – http://www.amazon.com

Publish your own CDs, DVDs, video downloads, and Amazon MP3s.

amazon.com

E-mail and Newsletters

E-mail and newsletters pertain to your list of clientele whether they are buyers, sellers, or non-clients. This is about maintaining a relationship with the people you come in contact with online and offline. Forward them information consistently, as written on your Internet marketing schedule, but not annoyingly.

MLS/IDX Provider

iNeedIDX – http://www.ineedidx.com

iNeedIDX provides real estate agents, real estate teams and real estate offices a way to automatically display Multiple Listing Service (IDX/MLS) Property Listings on their company websites and blogs.

Press Releases

PRWeb – http://www.prweb.com

Press release distribution helps you create buzz, increase online visibility, and drive website traffic. Learn how to send your first release today.

PR Newswire – http://www.prnewswire.com

PR Newswire's news distribution, targeting, monitoring, and marketing solutions help you connect and engage with target audiences across the globe.

Google News – http://news.google.com

Comprehensive up-to-date news coverage, aggregated from sources all over the world by Google News.

Yahoo! News – http://news.yahoo.com

The latest news and headlines from Yahoo! News. Get breaking news stories and in-depth coverage with videos and photos.

Bing News – http://www.bing.com/news

News from around the world, national news, and local news sources, structured to give you in-depth coverage of sports, entertainment, business, politics, weather, and other news.

Social Media

Twitter – http://twitter.com

Instantly connect to what's most important to you. Follow your friends, experts, favorite celebrities, and breaking news. Most importantly, answer the question, "What are you doing?"

Google+ - http://plus.google.com

Google + aims to make sharing on the web more like sharing in real life. Check out Circles, Messenger, and Hangouts.

Facebook – http://www.facebook.com

Facebook is a social utility that connects people with friends and others who work, study, and live around them.

Myspace – http://www.myspace.com

Myspace is the leading social entertainment destination powered by the passion of fans. Music, movies, celebs, TV, and games made social.

Digg – http://digg.com

The best news, videos, and pictures on the web as voted on by the Digg community. Breaking news on technology, politics, entertainment, and more!

LinkedIn – http://www.linkedin.com

100 million+ members. Manage your professional identity, build and engage with your professional network, and access knowledge, insights, and opportunities.

Plaxo – http://www.plaxo.com

The leading smart address book, Plaxo unifies your contacts across sources, proactively updates contact info, and syncs your complete address book with other leading social media sites.

Flickr – http://www.flickr.com

Flickr is almost certainly the best online photo management and sharing application in the world. Show off your favorite photos and videos to the world.

FriendFeed – http://friendfeed.com

Allows you to build a customized feed made up of content your friends on other collaborative sites have shared, including news articles, photos, and more.

StumbleUpon – http://www.stubleupon.com

StumbleUpon is a discovery engine that finds the best of the web, recommended just for you.

reddit – http://www.reddit.com

User-generated news links. Votes promote stories to the front page.

Technorati – http://technorati.com

Real-time search for user-generated media, including weblogs, by tag or keyword. Also provides popularity indexes.

Technorati

Videos

YouTube – http://www.youtube.com

Share your videos with friends, family, and the world.

Broadcast Yourself™

Dailymotion – http://www.dailymotion.com

The latest music videos, short movies, TV shows, funny and extreme videos. Upload, share, and embed your videos.

TubeMogul – http://www.tubemogul.com

Video advertising built for branding. Real-time buying of video ads across millions of sites.

Vimeo – http://vimeo.com

Vimeo is a respectful community of creative people who are passionate about sharing the videos they make. They provide the best tools and highest quality video.

References

American Marketing Association, Resource Library, Dictionary, accessed January 5, 2011, http://www.marketingpower.com/_layouts/Dictionary.aspx?dLetter = B.

Banking.com staff. "Social Media Statistics: By-the-Numbers," July 2011, http://www.banking2020.com/2011/07/05/social-media-statistics-by-the-numbers-july-2011/.

Clark, Jerry. "Start a Blog with an Authority Website or Brand," *ABC Article Directory,* accessed January 2012, http://www.abcarticledirectory.com/Article/Start-a-Blog-with-an-Authority-Website-or-Brand/889161.

Darren Tunstall. "Blog." http://darrentunstall.com/.

Google Maps. Google, accessed January 2012, http://maps.google.com/.

Google Keyword Tool Google, accessed January 2012, http://www.googlekeywordtool.com/.

Hampton, Keith N., Lauren Sessions Goulet, Lee Rainie, Kristen Purcell. "Frequency of use for users of different social

networking site platforms," Social Networking Sites and Our
Lives, Pew Internet & American Life Project, June 16, 2011,
http://pewinternet.org/Reports/2011/Technology-and-social-
networks.aspx.

Hampton, Keith N., Lauren Sessions Goulet, Lee Rainie, Kristen
Purcell. "Education distribution by social networking site
platforms," Social Networking Sites and Our Lives, Pew Internet
& American Life Project, June 16, 2011, http://pewinternet.org/
Reports/2011/Technology-and-social-networks.aspx.

Klein, Karen E. "A Practical Guide to Branding," *Adminsecret,*
accessed January 2012, http://adminsecret.monster.com/
benefits/articles/464-a-practical-guide-to-branding.

Milgram, Stanley. *Obedience to Authority.* New York: Harper &
Row, Publishers, Inc., 1974.

MLS.com. MLS Multiple Listing Service Listings, accessed January
2012, http://www.mls.com/.

National Association of Realtors. *2010 NAR Profile of Home Buyers
and Sellers.* Chicago: National Association of Realtors, 2010.

Robbins, Anthony. *Awake the Giant Within: How to Take
Immediate Control of Your Mental, Emotional, Physical and
Financial Destiny!* New York: Free Press, 1991.

Wikipedia. "La Jolla." Accessed January 2012, http://en.wikipedia.
org/wiki/La_Jolla.

WordPress.org. WordPress. Accessed January 2012, http://
wordpress.org/.

Yelp. Accessed January 2012, http://www.yelp.com/.

Index

Made in the USA
Lexington, KY
08 April 2013